Praise for Steve Deace and *Rules for Patriots*

"As a frequent guest on the *Steve Deace Show,* I know that when it comes to taking on the radical left and the Obama agenda, Steve Deace is without peer. We need more folks like Steve who are fearless in their advocacy for protecting the freedoms and liberties that make this country great. Buy his book—you won't regret it."

—CHRIS CHOCOLA, President, Club for Growth

"Clear-eyed and lion-hearted, Steve Deace is a latter-day Sam Adams. Every grassroots citizen who cherishes freedom and justice should study this highly readable antidote to political despair. These brilliant rules for political combat, if consistently wielded by an 'irate, tireless minority,' will undoubtedly save our country."

—DEAN CLANCY, Vice President of Public Policy, FreedomWorks

"The American people, increasingly frustrated with the loss of liberty and expansion of government, are offered a tough burst of honesty and clarity from Steve Deace—whether it is on air or in his book. Steve shines the light on the Republican Party establishment and offers encouragement that 'we the people' can take our country back."

—RAFAEL CRUZ, father of U.S. Senator Ted Cruz (R-TX)

"Republicans are relying on Democrats to lose elections instead of trying to win with a mandate. Steve Deace presents some great 'Rules for Patriots' to start winning with conservative conviction."

—ERICK ERICKSON, RedState and Fox News Contributor

"You will never think about the challenges to America the same after you read Steve Deace."

—NEWT GINGRICH, Former House Speaker and *New York Times* best-selling author

"Steve Deace has authored a superb primer for conservatives who want to win. Whether you are considering running for office, a member of your local Tea Party, or a concerned citizen debating the issues of the day, this book is a must read."

—MARK LEVIN, syndicated radio host

"In *Rules for Patriots,* Steve Deace lays out a blue print for victory for conservatives - a blueprint based on drawing stark contrasts rather than painting in shades of gray. Deace calls for conservatives to fight rather than retreat, recognizing that without a fight, the Left will never back down."

—BEN SHAPIRO, *New York Times* best-selling author, *Breitbart, Truth Revolt*

"If you want to be able to say 'you're fired' to the people plunging this great country of ours down the drain, this book is for you. Steve Deace is one of the rising stars in conservative media, and he's able to tackle serious subject matter in a winsome way that's so easy to understand, even a Washington, D.C. politician can get it."

—DONALD TRUMP, American business magnate

"One thing is for certain, Steve Deace will never be confused with Joel Osteen. In *Rules for Patriots* Steve lays out the good, the bad and the ugly on the condition of our country and then lays out a game plan for conservatives to regain a real place on impact on the culture including politics."

—TIM WILDMON, President, American Family Association

"Steve Deace has given us a punchy indictment of a Republican Party establishment that seems bent on losing again in 2016 with another Dole-style automaton. Deace's own plan for victory will enrage the hacks and hangers-on, which is why normal Americans will love it."

—THOMAS WOODS, *New York Times* best-selling author

RULES FOR PATRIOTS

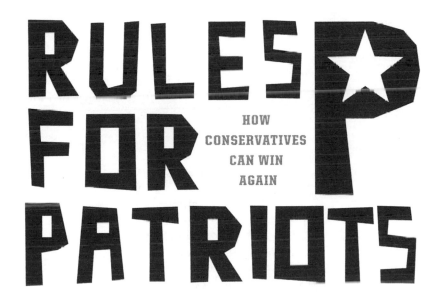

RULES FOR PATRIOTS

HOW CONSERVATIVES CAN WIN AGAIN

STEVE DEACE

WITH FOREWORD BY DAVID LIMBAUGH

POST HILL PRESS

Post Hill
PRESS

Published by Post Hill Press
109 International Drive, Suite 300
Franklin, TN 37067

Cover design by Ryan Truso
Interior book design by Neuwirth & Associates, Inc.

Visit us online at http://posthillpress.com

CONTENTS

FOREWORD

BY DAVID LIMBAUGH

I have been involved in politics since I was a young boy, and passionate about it for most of my life. My main focus has been on political philosophy and policy and not so much on the science of winning elections. I've often supported candidates, but I've never been a political operative or strategist. But that doesn't keep some people from assuming I'm knowledgeable about election strategy. After all, I've been writing a mostly political, nationally syndicated column for fifteen years so it's only natural people would make that assumption.

Based on that assumption, people often say to me, "This country is in such a mess. Everything is upside down and it keeps getting worse. Our culture has been overrun by those who believe wrong is right and right is wrong. Our governmental ruling class continues to expand government, drive us into national bankruptcy, abuse the Constitution and destroy our liberties, yet we can't seem to do anything about it. Most people I talk to agree that we are going in the wrong direction, but we keep losing elections anyway.

Even when we win, we don't make much progress in pushing back the government. You deal with this stuff everyday, David, so please tell me what we can do to stop this madness. Tell me what I can do to make a difference. I am not ready to give up on America. I will never give up on my children's future, but unless we find a way to turn this around their future doesn't look so bright. I am completely serious; I'm ready and willing to fight back. Just give me some direction."

To be completely honest with you, I've never had an adequate answer for these questions. Believe me, if I had a magical solution for turning things around I'd be shouting it out from the rooftops. I have some ideas, but they are broad philosophical points rather than a point-by-point strategy for winning elections.

My usual response is that first we have to stand up for the principles we believe in and express them unapologetically, even if the environment we're in makes that difficult. We have to encourage true conservatives to run for office—people who believe in the ideas of limited government and maximizing our political liberties. Quality people who are not just one-dimensional candidates, but who endorse all three legs of Ronald Reagan's three-legged stool: economic conservatism, social conservatism and foreign policy conservatism. This isn't to say that we have to be uncompromising purists or that we want to exclude from our tent those who don't agree with us on everything, but generally we should cultivate and encourage leaders who are comprehensively conservative.

Not only is it best for our nation that we support principled conservatives, but it is, in most cases, the best strategy for winning national elections. Polling has repeatedly shown that twice as many Americans self-identify as conservatives than as liberals. But we're not going to capitalize on that if we don't offer voters candidates who represent a true alternative to the nightmare of galloping statism from the ruling class. By supporting genuine conservatives who believe in the principles that have made America great, we will fire up and intensify our grassroots conservative base. We will energize people to vote because they will understand that their vote will make a difference in the direction of this country, instead of being wasted on a GOP candidate who talks the small-government talk, but ends governing like a Democrat.

I don't buy into the conventional wisdom preached by establishment Republicans that we must soften our message, or abandon social issues, in order to win independents, and that we must support milquetoast moderates because we won't be able to change anything unless we first get Republicans elected.

In the first place, I refuse to concede that Reagan conservatism is extremism or that it won't appeal to a substantial majority of the American people, if clearly and passionately articulated. America may well be drifting to the left, but timeless conservative policies are still the best formula for restoring prosperity, reversing our exploding debt, and making America stronger.

Notice that Democrats never preach bipartisanship, except when they're lecturing Republicans and seeking to shame them into joining them in further growing the government. The so-called bipartisan proposals never result in the rolling back of government or actual cuts in federal spending. Democrats never modulate their own ideas, which truly are extreme, and they keep winning national elections anyway. The Democratic presidential candidate has won the popular vote in five out of the last six presidential elections. This, despite the fact that the GOP has nominated moderates rather than conservatives in those elections, from George H. W. Bush, to Bob Dole, to George W. Bush to John McCain, to Mitt Romney.

I tell people that in addition to nominating and supporting like-minded candidates, we must have the courage to stand up for our convictions personally, instead of pretending things are just fine and that our positions won't make much difference. We shouldn't be abrasive or strident, but we need people to understand that we believe these are matters of grave importance and that we shouldn't just leave the political discussion to the politicians, pundits, and strategists. If we succumb to apathy or the cynical resignation that nothing we do will make a difference, we will, through our silence, be contributing to the demise of our nation and the destruction of our children's future.

Beyond expressing these general ideas, I find myself woefully inadequate at providing a specific roadmap for conservative electoral victories. I repeat: I am not an expert in political strategy and I am short on advice on the particulars. But I'm also aware that many of those who are knowledgeable in electoral strategy and tactics, even those on the political right, tend to be more interested in winning for winning's sake or for the advancement of their careers, as opposed to advancing substantive conservative ideas. I am not comfortable turning our future over to soulless political hired guns more interested in the game than in America's future.

I have long hoped that we could find a person representing the best of both worlds: a principled conservative with his finger on the pulse of the modern culture and savvy in both substantive policy and electoral strategy. Does any such person exist on our side—one who believes in America and who knows how to fight as effectively as a cutthroat liberal operative, but without compromising his convictions or operating unethically?

Let's face it; liberal Democrats have an advantage in politics because they generally subscribe to the view that the end justifies the means. They're all too willing to employ unethical means to achieve what they misperceive to be virtuous ends. Obama is the quintessential ends-justifies-means politician, who was trained at the feet of community organizing guru Saul Alinsky, whose "Rules for Radicals" has been his bible for demonizing opponents, winning elections, and advancing the radical progressive agenda, even though his progressive ideas have been minority ideas.

Is there no way we conservatives can win against such ruthlessness without abandoning our own principles and campaigning as unethically as our opponents? Do we have to fight hellfire with hellfire? Perish that thought. We mustn't surrender to the notion that we cannot compete against evil without becoming evil ourselves. We must remain confident that superior and nobler ideas will prevail if properly presented—that the truth will set us free.

We must also reject the hackneyed advice that we must choose between pragmatism and principle. There has to be a pragmatic strategy for winning while proudly proclaiming, rather than running from, our principles. That sounds nice, but there's a world of difference between instinctively believing there is such a principled strategy and actually knowing what it is.

Enter my friend, Steve Deace, with his "Rules for Patriots" in hand. When he asked me to read his book and consider writing a foreword for it, I had no idea what his prescriptions were.

Frankly, I've talked to a lot of smart people who've analyzed the 2012 election and our current political predicament and have proposed a number of intriguing ideas for Republicans to recapture the majority. But in my view, Steve Deace is the only one who is presenting the right blend of ideas—a blueprint for victory that is brilliantly strategic, smartly tactical, and yet grounded in, rather than compromising our conservative principles. There is no conflict between Deace's strategic proposals and the articulation and advancement of principled conservatism, precisely because his strategic proposals are steeped in these principles themselves.

We need to learn, says Deace, how to "win to govern, instead of governing to win." But establishment Republicans, he notes, believe "you win to lead," while the grassroots understand that "you lead to win." The establishment side, sadly, has controlled the consultant class and there has been "a void among consultants who thought it was their job to help the conservative candidate persuade voters to his principles, as opposed to consultants persuading conservative candidates to water down their principles to appease the masses." What a refreshing perspective.

Steve is a nationally syndicated radio talk show host based in Iowa, the state that always has the first GOP presidential caucus, giving him "a bird's eye view of the how the sausage gets made" and an opportunity "to meet many of the politicians, pundits, consultants, journalists and movers and shakers" involved in the process. This "unique opportunity" has given him a perspective that others might not have to "see what works and what does not. To see why candidates falter and fail, and why they thrive and succeed."

Drawing on this experience, Deace developed a ten-point approach for conservatives running for elective office, which he calls "Deace's 10 Commandments of Political Warfare," and which he presents and explains in this book. Finally, a "how to" book for conservatives and Republicans based on the Biblical injunction that we be as wise as serpents and as innocent as doves. Deace shows that we can be as savvy and effective as Clinton war room thugs without adopting their amoral tactics.

Having just turned 40, Steve is in a better position than some of us to understand what's going on with the younger generations. He understands that the culture is influencing politics more than politics is influencing culture and he has tailored his ideas accordingly. He understands that it is difficult to persuade people of ideas that at are at odds with their own worldview and so recommends that we develop long-term strategies to make significant inroads into the culture, the public schools and universities. But he also recognizes that worldview evangelism is a long-term proposition—that it's going to take years to reverse these trends that have been years in the making. Obviously, we can't afford to wait for years to start winning elections. We must begin to do this immediately.

How do we do that? Deace points out that Obama won young voters, even though they've been the group hardest hit by his policies—they'll bear the brunt of this debilitating debt he's created. But we aren't succeeding in winning them over by broad appeals to values, like Judeo-Christian morality and limited government, because these ideas don't resonate with them, given their education and background. Instead of wooing them with abstract values, we need to offer them concrete solutions. "When someone's self-interest is at stake, solutions trump values every time." We need to show them how our policies will make their lives better—directly. And we're not making that case.

But before we can successfully present proposed solutions for our many problems we have to overcome another daunting obstacle. The Republican Party is the existing vehicle for advancing a conservative agenda and its platform is based on traditional values and ideas that have made America unique. But at this point, the powerbrokers of the Republican Party often stand in the way of conservative ideas, rather than promoting them.

The Republican Party establishment has shown great resistance to grassroots conservatives and to conservative leaders who refuse to place their allegiance to party above their conservative principles. Deace has dubbed the Republican ruling class "Republicrats," which he says, aren't much different from Democrats. They pretend to be conservatives by paying lip service to conservative principles. But they are even worse than so-called RINOs (Republicans in name only), because at least RINOs openly campaign and govern from the middle-left. Republicrats are sneakier because they campaign as conservatives, but then proceed to govern from the middle-left. Indeed, they devote more energy and resources to fighting grassroots conservatives and the tea party than they do in opposing Democrats. "Instead of being excited by an energized base," he says, they [are] threatened by it."

Deace says that in order to understand why the nation continues to be governed from the left despite the majority of Americans leaning to the right, we must understand that there are three primary languages used in contemporary American politics. People either speak in plain English, politically correct speech, or in a technocratic dialect—the latter being the vernacular of the "Republicrat ruling class." This dialect, argues, Deace, is used to fool conservatives into supporting establishment Republican candidates who are anything but conservative. Deace identifies ten phrases most often used by Republicrats to pull off this linguistic deception and tells us how to recognize it for what it is.

Deace is correct about the Republican establishment's resistance to the conservative agenda. The establishment wing of the Republican Party tells us we have to avoid an impasse with President Obama and his Democratic congress at every turn, because, for example, if the government shuts down as a result of this impasse, no matter how much it may be the Democrats' fault, the Republicans will be blamed for it. We're told we have to surrender short of shutting the government down, even if it means piling on the national debt, continuing to ignore entitlements, increasing taxes, and gutting the military.

The GOP establishment almost always ends up capitulating, more or less, to the Obama liberals, arguing that we're impotent until we win the next election. "It's simply the best we can do for now and we must keep our powder dry for the next election. If we fight too hard, we'll look like extremists and lose the next election." For them, it's always about the next election. And we continue to lose every such "next election" by following their fecklessness. In the meantime, for good measure, the establishment demonizes and vilifies those bold patriots like Sen. Ted Cruz and Sen. Mike Lee, who insist on standing up to Obama in the here and now and not waiting for the mythical panacea of the "next election."

Deace offers concrete and effective ideas for nominating and electing principled conservative Republicans over the opposition of both establishment Republicans and Democrats. He does not recommend cashiering the Republican Party in favor of a third party, but taking back the party from within, then using it—as it was intended—to advance the ideas of its base, which is decidedly conservative. The answer is not to acquiesce in the Republican Party's movement to the left under the leadership of Republicrats who have contempt for the party's very base, but to recapture it and turn it around.

At some points in this book, Deace is very hard hitting against certain establishment politicians and political operatives and I don't share his sometimes-harsh assessments in every case. But his specific ideas for recapturing the Republican Party for conservatism and for winning elections are thoughtful, and, I believe, immensely promising. It is about time that someone on our side, someone truly on our side who shares our convictions, presented us with a viable plan that has a real chance of making a difference in changing America's political class for the better. Steve Deace has done just that, with this provocative, smart, bold, innovative and powerful book.

RULES FOR PATRIOTS

INTRODUCTION

They shoved another establishment hack down our throats in 2012, and we lost again. The names change—George Ford or Mitt McDole—but the results remain the same. Disaster for the Republican Party, but far more importantly, disaster for the country.

Like many of you, I'm sadly not surprised, because the Republican Party has lost the popular vote in five of the last six elections. But that won't deter the Republican Party establishment from trying to snatch defeat from the jaws of victory yet again . . . and again . . . and again. Losing is in these people's DNA. They'll try to blow 2014 before we even get to 2016. The only reason they didn't blow 2010 is because the Tea Party, God bless 'em, dragged them kicking and screaming across the finish line.

If we're going to stop them from blowing more elections, and thus finishing off whatever is left of our beloved Constitutional republic, we're going to need as many people as possible to read this book.

See, the very same people that have shoved these "electable" losers down our throats for decades now have re-emerged from their beltway spider holes to tell us that Mitt Romney lost because he was—get this—*too* conservative.

I know, I laughed out loud, too. Right before I realized the joke is really on us, our children, and our grandchildren—so this is really no laughing matter.

Now these same losers are saying we have to abandon whatever shred of principled conservatism actually still exists within the Republican Party leadership in order to win.

Yet we now know that is a pernicious lie.

Romney did everything the cynical Karl Rove wing of the party says Republicans have to do to win. He abandoned his base when he said[1] the grassroots uprising standing up for Chick-fil-a was "not a part of my campaign," and he joined the liberal dog pile on Todd Akin. He played it safe and didn't offer any major tax or entitlement reform ideas to avoid the fiscal cliff out of fear of being demagogued. He ran on platitudes and talked more about how bad President Obama is rather than what plans for the future he had. He even became the first Republican presidential nominee to ever run *pro-child killing* television ads,[2] which aired in battle-ground states like Virginia, Ohio and Iowa (all of which Romney lost, by the way). Romney also won over key independents in several battleground states.

And he still lost.

If anything good can come from getting our butts kicked in 2012, it's that we've finally been able to debunk several lies and clever myths of the Republican Party's wretched ruling class:

---

1 Charlie Spiering, "Romney: Chick-fil-a Controversy 'Not a Part of My Campaign'," Washington Examiner, August 3, 2012, http://washingtonexaminer.com/romney-chick-fil-a-controversy-not-part-of-my-campaign/article/2503932

2 Billy Hallowell, "New Romney Ad Targets Women: Abortion Should Be an Option in Certain Cases," *The Blaze*, October 17, 2012, http://www.theblaze.com/stories/2012/10/17/new-romney-ad-targets-women-abortion-should-be-an-option-in-certain-cases/

Lie and clever myth #1: Republicans lose elections because they're too conservative so independents side with Democrats.

TRUTH: Romney won independent voters[3] in the crucial battleground states of Virginia and Ohio, two of the three states he had to win to win the presidency. In Florida, the other battleground state Romney had to have, he actually did 8 points better among independents than John McCain did in 2008. In Colorado[4] Romney won independents by seven points, after McCain lost independents in Colorado by eight points in 2008. Translation—Romney did exactly what he had to do with independents and still lost. Reverse the outcome in Colorado, Florida, Ohio, and Virginia, and Romney is elected President of the United States.

Lie and clever myth #2: Romney lost because of the GOP's alleged "war on women" so that means we can't be pro-life anymore.

TRUTH: What the GOP really has is a diversity problem.[5] White voters in every demographic—including women and young voters—voted for Romney. Let me repeat that: a majority of white voters regardless of age and gender voted Republican in the 2012 presidential election. Romney won *white women by 14 points*. A massive turnout of blacks and Latinos—the Democrat base—determined the election and gave Obama the support he needed to win. The Democrats won by doing a better job than the Republicans of turning out their base. Which leads me to my next point.

---

3 Matt Negrin, "Exit Polls: Obama's Winning Coalition of Women and Non-Whites," ABC News, November 6, 2012, http://abcnews.go.com/Politics/OTUS/exit-polls-independents-siding-romney-ohio-virginia/story?id=17656990

4 Brian Montopoli, "Exit Poll: Close Race in Colorado," CBS News, November 6, 2012, http://www.cbsnews.com/8301-250_162-57546124/exit-poll-close-race-in-colorado-pot -initiative-up/

5 David C. Wilson, "The Elephant in the Exit Poll Results," *Huffington Post*, November 8, 2012, http://www.huffingtonpost.com/david-c-wilson/the-elephant-in-the-exit_b _2094354.html

Lie and clever myth #3: The Republicans energized their base, but it's just shrinking so the party has to move left.

TRUTH: Promises that a swing of 17 million Evangelicals that didn't vote in 2008 would show up and swing the 2012 election in Romney's favor never panned out[6].

The reality is 2.5 million *fewer* Evangelicals voted in 2012 than 2008. Fewer Catholics voted in 2012 than 2008 as well, despite the presence of two Catholic vice presidential candidates. 6.4 million Evangelicals actually voted *for* Obama. In the crucial battleground state of Ohio, Obama actually *improved* his white Evangelical turnout by 8% compared to 2008. I'm sure much of that is due to Obama's bailout of the auto industry there (which didn't stop Detroit from going bankrupt),[7] but Romney running pro-child killing television ads probably didn't endear him to pro-life voters. Romney also ran those pro-child killing television ads in Virginia, and CNN's exit polls found the Evangelical turnout there declined by 7% compared to 2008.

Yes, Romney did get the same hefty percentage of Evangelical voters that George W. Bush got in his victorious 2004 campaign, but the turnout wasn't large enough. Apparently all the efforts to distort Romney's far left record as governor of Massachusetts, and make him into some kind of conservative superhero at the same time he's shunning his base and flip-flopping on their issues, didn't pay off.

Finally, get this: Romney even did *worse* among his fellow Mormons than George W. Bush did in 2004,[8] if you can believe that.

---

6 Joel C. Rosenberg, "More than 6 Million Self-Described Evangelicals Voted for Obama. Why, and What Else Do the Exit Polls Tell Us About How Christians Voted?" November 8, 2012, http://flashtrafficblog.wordpress.com/2012/11/08/more-than-6-million-self-described-evangelicals-voted-for-obama-why-what-else-do-the-exit-polls-tell-us-about-how-christians-voted/

7 Conn Carroll, "Obama Lets Detroit Go Bankrupt," *Washington Examiner,* July 13, 2013, http://washingtonexaminer.com/morning-examiner-obama-lets-detroit-go-bankrupt/article/2533259

8 Jaweed Kaleem, "Religious Vote Data Shows Shift in Obama's Faith-Based Support," *Huffington Post,* November 8 2012, http://www.huffingtonpost.com/2012/11/07/obama-religion-voters-2012_n_2090258.html

Romney lost the election in the end because his base wasn't as energized as Obama's was. All the so-called "skewed" polling that pointed to an Obama turnout of Democrats similar to 2008 turned out to be correct. If you count the 2.5 million fewer Evangelicals that voted compared to 2008, and the 6.4 million Evangelicals that voted for Obama, a future Republican nominee has almost 9 million potential new voters in 2016 if he actually reaches out to them credibly and consistently.

Adding a plurality of those 9 million voters to Romney's 2012 coalition would make the Republican nominee virtually unbeatable in 2016 or any other future election. But to accomplish that feat he or she will have to make them feel welcome in the party, and assure them that he or she shares their courage of conviction.

But it's not just Evangelicals that are tired of voting *against* Democrats rather than voting *for* Republicans. They are just one segment of the at least 6 million people[9] that traditionally lean Republican and voted in 2008 but didn't vote in 2012. Then there were those that didn't stay home but cast a protest vote instead. Like the almost 45,000 liberty-loving Floridians that voted for Libertarian Party candidate Gary Johnson, and provided sixty percent of Obama's 2012 margin for victory in that swing state. Then there's the emerging Libertarian influence within the GOP cultivated by Ron and Rand Paul. These people are tired of voting for a lesser form of socialism under the Republican Party banner, and several of them I know were "Ron Paul or bust" voters in 2012. They never saw Romney as a true champion of limited government, so they didn't vote for him.

Persistent attempts in the future to sell these patriots on milquetoast, or to scare them into voting against dastardly Democrats, may result in those doing the selling being handsomely rewarded by the Republican ruling class. But it likely will result in more of them staying home and thus another Republican election loss.

The real numbers show people are growing increasingly tired of

---

9 Dan McLaughlin, "Fear of the Missing White Voter," *Red State,* July 17, 2013, http://www.redstate.com/2013/07/17/fear-of-the-missing-white-voters/

being asked to cast votes they know they won't be proud of later. As frustration with the status quo grows huge names like Sarah Palin are[10] openly talking about the possibility of a third party, as is one of the biggest conservative websites in the country.[11]

Modernization of the Republican Party is one thing, but moderation is another. Compromise is one thing, but capitulation is another.

What we need to do is make a list of everyone in the alleged "conservative media" that peddles party establishment propaganda, or went on Fox News guaranteeing a Romney victory and told us how skewed all the mainstream media polls were (when in the last three presidential elections they've been exactly right),[12] and resolve never to trust these false prophets again.

Frankly, we should have known better than to trust them in the first place. During the past two primary cycles didn't we watch many of these same people tell us Mike Huckabee was a Christian socialist, Ron Paul was a certifiable nut-case, Rick Santorum was a pro-life statist, and Newt Gingrich opposed the very Reagan Revolution he was a foot soldier in? Meanwhile, the establishment choice—Willard Romney—could tip-toe between the raindrops without getting wet.

The people trashing and slandering non-establishment candidates in primaries are the very same people that tell conservatives we have to be team players (see that as stand for nothing). And yet they attack us like they would never attack liberals. Perhaps if Romney had gone after the president in the final two debates on Benghazi the way he went after Gingrich and Santorum in the primary, he wouldn't have lost the election.

---

10 Steve Deace, "Palin's Provocative Proposal: A Cost Benefit Analysis of Conservatives Leaving the GOP," *Townhall,* July 6, 2013, http://townhall.com/columnists/stevedeace/2013/07/06/palins-provocative-proposal-a-costbenefit-analysis-of-conservatives-leaving-the-gop-n1632357/page/full

11 Erick Erickson, "There Will Be a Third Party," *Red State,* July 29, 2013, http://www.redstate.com/2013/07/29/we-will-have-a-third-party/

12 Steve Deace, "Lies, Darned Lies, and Polls," *Townhall,* November 3, 2012, http://townhall.com/columnists/stevedeace/2012/11/03/lies_darned_lies_and_polls

But now it's time to move forward.

I recently spoke to a group of grassroots conservative activists at the Institute on the Constitution in Baltimore, and shared with them that I believe we are a movement in a generational transition. On one hand there is the Reagan generation, and my generation on the other.

The Reagan generation sees how much freedom and liberty has been lost since Reagan, and are trying to do whatever they can to hold on to whatever is left before it's completely lost. The hope is that if we hold on long enough and defeat Democrats with any (and by "any" we sadly mean "any") Republican, we can create another perfect storm that gave rise to Reagan in the first place and it will be "morning in America" again.

My generation doesn't have that nostalgia for the Reagan era, because we were growing up and not really paying attention, or weren't even born at all. Now that we are paying attention, we don't see the country in the context of what has been lost but rather how much ground needs to be gained. We are not seeing this purely in the context of the next election cycle. We're seeing this in a generational cycle, which is why we oppose compromises on important issues like life and the debt ceiling. We don't really care what the ruling class and its brigade of hand-wringers masquerading as pundits and pollsters think, because we're the ones that will pick up the long-term tab for the financial, moral, and spiritual brokenness of the country long after they're six feet under.

We're looking at the next 40 years, not just the next four.

Ironically, though we may not be a part of the Reagan generation, we have the same perspective Reagan had in 1976 when he said the Republican Party ought to stand for something other than becoming more like Democrats, and there should be no more "pale pastels" but "bold colors" instead.

Eventually my generation is going to get its chance to lead because we have time on our side. Nobody lives forever. When we do get our chance to lead, and it may be sooner rather than later, we need to learn the lessons of recent failures lest we fail our children and grandchildren.

This election provided plenty of hard lessons, but also a useful road map of how to win the future:

1. The truth still sets us free.

Yes, the mainstream media favors liberals, but just giving our yin to their yang doesn't produce truth—it just produces another echo chamber. I couldn't believe how many conservatives I know and trust who really thought Romney was going to win, and win convincingly, despite the fact several polling models with a 96% accuracy rate in the past two presidential elections said otherwise.[13]

Our version of propaganda is no truer than their version of propaganda.

I say this in love, but brothers and sisters, some of our brethren are dangerously close to becoming the magically thinking, virtual reality-living creatures we accuse the Democrat base of being. If we want to advance truth, we need to believe the truth ourselves—even when it's inconvenient. And the truth is we are no longer the dominant view in the culture, and we have some work to do to change that.

2. Hypocrisy doesn't sell.

Pollster Scott Rasmussen once told me the single most unpopular piece of legislation in recent American history was the (in my opinion criminal) TARP bailout of 2008. Yet we nominated a candidate who was for it in the next presidential election. Good luck going to Toledo and telling Ohioans making $15/hour who think their job was saved by the auto industry bailout that they didn't deserve a government handout, but Merrill Lynch and Goldman Sachs did. Sometimes we just write the Democrats' commercials for them.

---

13 Steve Deace, "Morning Briefing," October 31, 2012, http://stevedeace.com/news/national-politics/morning-briefing-october-31st-2012/

3. Cast a vision.

After the Democrats lost an election in 2004 they probably shouldn't have lost, the more principled-progressive wing of the party took over. The result was an anti-Bush liberal uprising in 2006 similar to the anti-Obama Tea Party uprising of 2010. Next, the new progressives defeated the more pragmatic Clintons head-to-head in a presidential primary. Obama ran for president promising his base he would move the ball down the field for them with their crown jewel legislation—Obamacare. He then went right back to that base in 2012 and worked the exact same get-out-the-vote model that worked in 2008.

He embraced his base, even on social issues, both in the White House and at his convention. While we were scoffing at him for never moderating, Obama was energizing his base all along in preparation for a tough re-election. The progressives cast a vision that took more than one election cycle, followed it through, and won. They never detoured no matter what the facts were on the ground because they have a courage of their conviction that their vision is what's best for the country. They wanted to win to govern. The Republican ruling class wants to govern to win. The Democrats want to run a country. The Republican ruling class wants to run a party.

4. Stop demonizing our neighbors.

We called Bill Clinton every name in the book and even impeached him, and that didn't work. We called Obama every name in the book (some of them were even true), and all we did was help him to portray his failures as Bush's fault and energize his base all the more. We called Sandra Fluke a "slut" and all we did was scare even more skittish advertisers away from conservative talk radio.

Yes, there is a double standard here. You should see some of the Tweets I received after appearing on MSNBC, like when someone tweeted he hoped my daughters would get raped after I defended former U.S. Senate candidate Richard Mourdock. We watch homosexual activists glitter bomb conservatives and can only imagine what would happen if we returned such fire. It's not fair, but it is what it is.

I am as fiery as the next guy, and at times have not been able to hold my tongue, especially when it's fun not to. But I've learned that while we don't need to moderate our principles we do need to temper our approach. Ann Coulter-shrillness may sell books to the already-converted, but it's losing the culture at-large. Yes, the entire Sandra Fluke controversy was a phony, liberal media meme devised to minimize the influence of Limbaugh, the Godfather of conservative media.

But that proves my point.

While we have focused on political results, the Left has focused on changing culture. Culture is the mouth of the river. Politics is what occurs downstream. We wait to battle them on the political level, but by then it's too late because they have already coordinated their assets in media, pop culture, and technology to create the perception of a narrative. Whether it's phony or not is irrelevant, because the media *is* the message. As Lenin once famously said, "Repeat a lie often enough and it becomes the truth."

As a result of surrendering culture to the Left, we no longer have a country that accepts many of our premises. Thus we have to go into—pardon the phrase—evangelism mode. That requires a relationship and trust, and it's hard to build that rapport with people while demonizing them. Pardon the cliché, but we need happy warriors. As D.L. Moody once said, "When you're winsome you win some."

Most of our neighbors we are angry with for voting the way they did don't go to church. Most of them were taught things about this country in government (no longer public) schools that are contrary to this nation's actual history. How should we expect them to vote given those circumstances? Nobody can rise above their own worldview. People can only act on that which they believe to be true. Since the 1960s we have surrendered academia and pop culture to statists and social Darwinists with nary a shot fired. What did we think would be the generational result of that abrogation?

We're not a silent majority anymore. We're a dwindling plurality in clear and present danger of becoming a *silenced* minority. If you want your neighbors to vote differently, then we have to change their worldview.

5. We need solutions—not just values.

Obama won young voters again despite the fact they're the group hardest hit by his policies. They will be saddled with all the debt we're tacking on, and live in a more dangerous world in the long run with the emergence of the Arab Spring, the Muslim Brotherhood, and eventually a nuclear Iran.

We are losing them by trying to win them over to values that make freedom possible—Judeo-Christian morality, personal responsibility, limited government, etc.—yet they have been educated in an environment that makes these values foreign to them. It only will get harder to win them over as they get older. For example, they have not been taught the Second Amendment is required for keeping individual freedom secure from government tyranny, but rather gun control as a means of stopping little children from being killed by gang violence or gun accidents.

See, they're not looking for *values*, they're looking for *solutions*.

For better or for worse, there is one Republican who has been attracting younger voters in the past two presidential primaries, and that was Ron Paul. Granted, some are young people whose only goal seems to be legalizing marijuana, but that's also a lazy stereotype on the part of too many of my fellow conservatives.

Many of them are critically-thinking young people who don't understand why it's their responsibility to pay for the lack of fiscal and moral discipline of their forefathers, and why they have to die in foreign lands nation-building when our nation is declining here. Dr. Paul offered them *solutions* to these problems and not just *values*. I don't agree with all of Dr. Paul's solutions, but I do think we could learn from his approach.

Do we have a *solution* for these young voters to their problems? Furthermore, do we have *solutions* to the problems with healthcare and job creation that middle class voters think much more about than they do the deeper moral crisis in the country? Changing worldviews is a long-term goal, but in the short-term we can still win elections by coming up with real *solutions* to people's problems as opposed to a general philosophical discussion around *values*.

When someone's self-interest is at stake, *solutions* trump *values* every time.

Case in point: There are working class whites in Ohio who helped George W. Bush win the state twice and John Kasich get elected governor in 2010, but they went for Obama in 2012. They didn't see him as a statist putting us on the road to being the next Greece. They saw Obama as the guy that saved daddy's job at the Chrysler plant and thus kept food on the family's table. Similarly, after the 2006 conflict with Israel that it instigated, Islamic terrorist organization Hezbollah started handing out cash to Lebanese[14] families whose homes were destroyed by Israeli bombing.

Again, solutions trump values when self-interest is at stake.

6. We're too white.

African-Americans routinely vote with us on an issue like marriage, yet there is almost never any Republican Party follow-up with them after they do. Romney did worse with Latinos than John McCain did in 2008. The reality is the country is becoming less white, so we're going to have to come up with ways to apply our principles to the needs of non-whites like never before.

It doesn't mean we have to pander to them or try to out amnesty the Democrats, because that will just result in the loss of more liberty and the further erosion of the conservative base (which, frankly, the GOP establishment might want), but it means we may need to take a more measured approach on some hot-button issues.

---

14 "Hezbollah Pays Out $12K in Cash to Lebanese Who Lost Their Homes," Fox News, August 18, 2006, http://www.foxnews.com/story/2006/08/18/hezbollah-pays-out-12k-in-us-cash-to-lebanese-who-lost-their-homes/

For example, how can we demand that minorities stop seeing government as their primary vehicle to access the American dream when Republicans in the corporate class do it all the time? To ask African-Americans to totally abandon programs like affirmative-action, and Latinos to look the other way while we mass deport some of their family members and friends is unrealistic when we allow Republicrats to get away with using government for their purposes all the time.

I've said it before but I'll say it again: sometimes it's like we're writing the Democrats' campaign commercials for them.

Look at Texas,[15] one of the most Republican and conservative states in the country. About 38% of the state's population is Latino, so how are conservatives making gains in a state with such a huge Latino population, and can it be modeled nationally? No one would accuse Texas of being a moderate state—far from it. Most of us consider it conservative Valhalla, so why not follow its lead?

7. Pro-lifers need a plan for ultimate victory.

Please stop quoting polls telling me the country is more pro-life than ever before. When Richard Mourdock loses a U.S. Senate seat in a very Republican state for saying that all life, regardless of how it's conceived, is a gift from God and deserves to be protected, then that means we need to be honest with ourselves and stop believing our own fundraising propaganda.

Pro-lifers are the largest and most loyal voting bloc the GOP has, yet we have almost nothing to show for it except the carcass of Todd Akin abandoned on the side of the road by the GOP establishment. Akin is not a victim of his own mangled remarks voters held him accountable for. But we were victimized by a party establishment who decided three months before the election they'd rather have Harry Reid as Majority Leader than a good man with

---

15 "Quick Facts: Texas Census," United States Government, July 20, 2013, http://quickfacts.census.gov/qfd/states/48000.html

a 96% American Conservative Union rating in the house, because there was no way to win the majority in the U.S. Senate in 2012 without winning Akin's race. There was plenty of time to rehabilitate Akin in a very Republican state, but the ruling class piled on him instead.

I was born to a 15-year old mom. I have members of my own family who were conceived via those so-called "exceptions" (rape, incest, life of the mother, fetal abnormality, etc.) that too many Republican Party politicians think are therefore okay to kill. If 40 years after *Roe v. Wade* the culture doesn't believe my own family line conceived in the horrific and traumatic circumstances pro-life pretenders call "exceptions" has the right to live, then we have lost the most crucial moral debate of this age and need to completely re-evaluate what we're doing and why we're doing it.[16]

Yet despite all of this, I remain optimistic.

God is still on the throne. My Savior lives. More and more patriots are waking up. This is still the greatest nation on earth. Providence has allowed us to live in a nation where we can at least somewhat control our own destiny. And liberty can flourish again if we have the same courage of conviction demonstrated by past generations that gave us the freedom we currently enjoy.

They that have ears to hear, let them hear.

While we're not out of time yet, like many of you the Left accuses of bitterly clinging to your guns and your Bibles, I believe the clock is ticking on these United States of America.

We cannot sustain this moral, financial, and spiritual bankruptcy much longer. Each day I do my radio program in acknowledgement of that inconvenient truth. That sense of urgency, amplified by the fact I am also one of the youngest nationally-syndicated talk show hosts and raising small children at home, is what makes our show sound a little different than most others.

See, I'm broadcasting out of a need greater and an instinct more

---

16 Steve Deace, "Abortion and the Conscience of a Nation," *Townhall,* October 13, 2012, http://townhall.com/columnists/stevedeace/2012/10/13/abortion _and _the _conscience_of_a_nation

basic than generating ratings, becoming wealthy, or even doing my part to win elections. Not that there is anything necessarily wrong with any of those things, or that I'm not motivated at least somewhat by them as well. I am human and an American after all, and also male, which means I'm competitive. But those motivations pale in comparison to my prime directive— leaving behind a better future for my children and grandchildren.

It's also why I am not shy about discussing on the airwaves the integral role faith played in founding this constitutional republic (as well as my own worldview), and the fact that without returning to that faithful foundation we have no future. At the start of my program each day we summarize our priorities this way: fear God, tell the truth, and (then) make money.

I am one of the first grassroots, everyday American patriots from the emerging and more, shall we say, *confrontational* Right to be granted a platform of this magnitude. Most of the other well-meaning, successful, and talented folks in my industry come from an era when the differences between the two political parties were quite stark in the minds of most and it was clearly "us" (Republicans) vs. "them" (Democrats). Now the "us" vs. "them" has completely changed. It's no longer Republicans vs. Democrats like it used to be. It's now the ruling class in both political parties vs. the American people.

I come from a generation that has witnessed a murky blurring of the lines, so I am not afflicted with any nostalgic myopia. This emerging, more confrontational Right is about driving issues first, not personalities or political parties. We don't believe there's any more time left for partisan games or kicking the can down the road. Either we will commit to the right course of action and courage of conviction that will preserve this republic or we won't.

It's just that simple.

Like many of you, I want to win the future for my children and grandchildren, and I don't define winning as losing a little slower.

To win we first need to know what we're up against. Like the "Two Towers" in the *Lord of the Rings* trilogy that perpetuate evil in Middle Earth, the American Left is propped up by four pillars:

The child-killing industry: Abortion is the oldest and most lucrative revenue stream to the American Left. On average, about 4,000 babies are killed via abortion in America each day, and the average cost is about $500 per kill. That's $2 million dollars per day, and if you multiply that by 365 days a year you come up with a $730 million annual industry that produces a lot of potential Democratic Party donations from Planned Parenthood, the leading child-killer in the country.

Now you know why Democrats will sell-out racial and ethnic minorities as well as UAW or Teamster's workers they claim to represent, but never sell-out the child killers. There's gold in them dismembered babies.

Without access to the money produced by the child-killing industry, the American Left disintegrates. Especially when you realize that an organization like Planned Parenthood, in addition to being the largest child killer in our nation, is also a mechanism to divert millions of dollars to its political arm—the Planned Parenthood Action Fund—that is nothing less than a shill for liberal Democrat candidates and legislation.

The homosexual lobby: Although not as vast as the child-killing industry, through moguls like Tim Gill and David Geffen the homosexual lobby has become one of the biggest revenue streams for the American Left. Leftist cultural enclaves like Hollywood that are the most hostile to any form of Judeo-Christian moral tradition have embraced lifestyles healthier civilizations have traditionally referred to as immoral and discouraged. However, with the help of Hollywood liberals controlling most of the messages conveyed in pop culture nowadays, they are working hand-in-hand with one another to soften the American people's resolve to accept homosexuality as normal despite losing 89% of the referendums on the definition of marriage. In the press coverage of the 2012 presidential election, it was reported that one in six Democrat fundraising "bundlers" was homosexual.

Government Education: The government schools K-12, and on into college, have essentially become the youth ministry for secular progressives. It is here, with the aid of pop culture, that they have

established their feeder system to replenish their ranks every generation. As the long-time former attorney for the National Education
Association admitted at his retirement party in 2009,[17] "NEA and its
affiliates have been singled out because they are the nation's leading
advocates for the type of liberal economic and social agenda (conservatives) find unacceptable." Some, like David Horowitz and my
friend E. Ray Moore, have been sounding the clarion call to confront this for many years. But sadly it's fallen mainly on deaf ears
within the majority of the conservative movement. I know one major
Evangelical author and speaker who had a book manuscript rejected
by one of the biggest organizations in the conservative movement,
because in it he confronted the Leftist indoctrination in our schools.

Government Sector Employee Unions: This is the mobocracy the
American Left uses to intimidate Republicans into caving into more
big government, and groups like AFSCME provide the worker
bees/ground troops for the Left's army in the culture war. They are
the most dedicated foot soldiers they have, and why wouldn't they
be? If your livelihood depended solely on the continued growth of
government, you would be as well. Look at what the Left has delivered for them in states like California and Michigan.[18]

Education bureaucrats in Detroit don't have to worry about losing
their jobs despite the fact only 7% of the city's 8th graders are reading
proficient. That's right. I said 7%. As in a 93% failure rate. In 2009
the Detroit school district had the lowest scores ever recorded on
the national math proficiency test. If you produced those kinds of
results in your industry wouldn't you expect to be fired? By the way,
according to the *New York Times*,[19] 95% of Detroit school kids are
black. So it's obvious the Democrats have delivered on their promises to help the minority community. Or not.

---

17 https://www.youtube.com/watch?v=Ahb8rBMuDDs

18 Steve Deace, "An Open Letter to Michigan's Workers," *Townhall,* December 5, 2012,
http://townhall.com/columnists/stevedeace/2012/12/15/an-open-letter-to-michigans
-workers-n1465974

19 Michael Winerip, "For Detroit Schools Mixed Picture on Reforms," *New York
Times,* March 13, 2011, http://www.nytimes.com/2011/03/14/education/14winerip.
html?pagewanted=all&_r=2&

Then there's California, whose 245,000 government employees is easily the most in the nation. Those workers are paid an average annual salary of $60,317, plus a rather generous benefits package. In 2011 California taxpayers shelled out $963 million in overtime pay to state employees, which was more than the next seven states on the list combined. These are just some of the reasons why the average California state employee makes 30% more than the same job pays in the private sector.

There is no way to preserve freedom, liberty, and prosperity for future generations without confronting these four pillars of the welfare state. It's been a long time since conservatives, let alone Republicans, have truly threatened the Left's power base. Governor Scott Walker in Wisconsin has successfully taken on the government sector employee unions in his state, and may be the only Republican I can think of to successfully dismantle one of these four pillars. Some estimates are reporting AFSCME in Wisconsin has lost at least 40,000 members since Walker ended mandatory union dues.

Now you know why they have fought so hard to get rid of him. You know the difference between someone like Walker and someone like New Jersey Governor Chris Christie, who *National Review* admitted wasn't a conservative no matter how many times Ann Coulter tried to convince us otherwise.[20] Look at the way the Left has reacted to Walker, throwing everything but the kitchen sink at him.

On the other hand, while Christie shows some bravado at his town halls you don't see the Left trying to get rid of and intimidate him the way they are Walker. In fact, Christie played a pivotal role in aiding Obama's re-election.[21] Walker is really fighting these people, while Christie is just shadowboxing.

---

20 Laura Donovan, "Ann Coulter: This Country Needs Chris Christie," *Daily Caller,* February 16, 2011, http://dailycaller.com/2011/02/16/ann-coulter-this -country-needs -chris-christie/

21 Erica Ritz, "Six Months Later Gov. Christie Again Praising Obama for his Sandy Response," *The Blaze,* April 29, 2013, http://www.theblaze.com/stories/2013/04/29/ gov-christie-is-again-praising-obama-for-his-sandy-response/

At the time this book was being written, Louisiana Governor Bobby Jindal was attempting to duplicate Walker's leadership by dismantling the government education pillar in his state. Walker and Jindal are real examples of the type of leadership necessary for victory, as opposed to just slowing the rate of liberal growth most Republicans (and sadly even most conservatives) aspire to.

The anti-Constitutional monstrosity known as Obamacare will be a massive boon to government sector employee unions. Yet while you had some principled Republicans like U.S. Senators Ted Cruz and Mike Lee leading a movement to defund it once and for all, they were opposed by posers—and their ruling class human shields disguised as commentators on Fox News—who just wanted more empty and worthless votes to repeal it instead.

Republicans have voted more than 40 times to repeal Obamacare, knowing it would go nowhere since Obama is obviously not going to repeal his own signature bill. See, that's low-lying fruit. They believe you're so stupid that they can tell you they voted to repeal it, you'll be satisfied, and then they'll be off the hook for allowing its implementation. That's why the Republican majority in the House of Representatives, where the Constitution says all appropriations begin, have to defund Obamacare. It's the only way to stop it. It's not a tactic. It's a duty. But that's hard and might offend the ruling elite and liberal media.

So they'd rather just allow the biggest promotion of abortion—an unprecedented threat to religious liberty (just ask Hobby Lobby) and a bill that will raise health insurance premium rates by more than 30% according to the Associated Press[22]—take effect instead. After all, it's not like the ruling class needs to worry. They can just exempt themselves from some of Obamacare's more punitive provisions if they need to.[23]

---

22 Betsy Fores, "Study: Obamacare to Raise Individual Claim Costs By 32 Percent," *Daily Caller,* March 27, 2013, http://dailycaller.com/2013/03/27/study-obamacare-to-raise-individual-claim-costs-by-32-percent/

23 Paul Gigot, "Opinion: White House Gives Congress Obamacare Waiver," *Wall Street Journal,* August 5, 2013, http://online.wsj.com/article/SB10001424127887324635904578644202946287548.html

In a war, you cannot claim victory as long as the enemy's infrastructure is still in place. Winning happens when you've dismantled your opponent's infrastructure and forced them to unconditionally surrender. Walker has done that in Wisconsin, and Jindal undertook the same in Louisiana. Senators like Cruz and Lee are trying to do the same in Washington, D.C. Sadly, they are the precious few examples to cite.

When we get leaders like this, we need to do everything we can to encourage and assist them. We desperately need more leaders like them. I believe if you read and follow the 10 Commandments in this book, you will help these leaders finish the job they started, and help us generate more leaders willing to be as bold.

Unfortunately, the old guard accuses us of being "purists" (as if I, as a Christian, should be insulted by that) for demanding we actually try to win rather than just lose a little slower. But the reality is we're the ones being the most pragmatic. We believe we do not have another generation to waste on "four legs good, two legs bad" partisan (and hypocritical) silliness. This is now about the cultural equivalent to a survival instinct, and folks need to either lead or get out of the way.

It doesn't get any more pragmatic than being motivated by the most basic human instinct—survival. Besides, what the old guard defines as pragmatism is really defeatism at a slower, more comfortable pace (more on that later in this book).

We don't trust the leadership of the Republican Party any more than we trust the Democrats, but are pragmatically willing to use the GOP's infrastructure as the most convenient vehicle to engage the political system to fight for our freedom and liberty.

We do not believe there is any such thing as a "fiscal conservative" but there are only conservatives. "Fiscal conservatives" and "pro-life Democrats" are like unicorns—figments of our imagination. A fiscal conservative is code language for a materialist who just wants more mammon. David Barton at Wallbuilders has documented for years that the more staunchly pro-life and pro-family someone is, the more staunchly they stand for limited government. If you can't trust a politician to defend your life, you definitely can't trust them to defend your money. Besides, good luck slashing the size of government without defending the family, since the breakdown of the family is the impetus for the welfare state in the first place.

Not to mention the more immoral a people become the bigger the government always gets, because the first thing an immoral people want to avoid is paying for their own mistakes. A welfare state profits off the basis of bad behavior, and then cost shifts the bill to do those who make sound decisions.

We do not romanticize the Republicans as the good guys and the Democrats as the bad, but see the leadership of both parties as part of a ruling class (thank you Anthony Codevilla) that is more concerned with maintaining their own gravy train than honoring their sworn oaths to uphold and defend the Constitution of these United States.

We are the grassroots.

This grassroots perspective I bring to the airwaves each day is what enabled me, by the grace of God, to have one of the highest-rated afternoon drive programs in the history of the legendary radio station 1040-WHO in Des Moines, which boasts Ronald Reagan as its first sports director. It was this same perspective that then provided me an opportunity to become one of the youngest nationally-syndicated radio hosts in the nation.

That brings me to this book.

I live in the first-in-the-nation caucus state of Iowa, which provides me a bird's eye view of how the sausage gets made. I get to meet many of the politicians, pundits, consultants, journalists, and movers and shakers you see on TV or read about. I've been wooed by presidential candidates driving their tour buses down my residential street, calling my house, or taking my wife and I out to dinner. I get to see the process from the inside, warts and all. According to Fox News,[24] I'm the reason Mike Huckabee won the 2008 Iowa Caucuses. That may be at least slightly overblown, but I'll happily embrace the publicity nonetheless.

---

24 http://stevedeace.com/news/videos/fox-news-profiles-steve-deace/

Seeing politics played out on a national level in my own back-yard has provided me a unique opportunity to learn from some of the best and the worst. To see what works and what does not. To see why candidates falter and fail, and why they thrive and suc-ceed. Many of my friends have run for public office—everything from school board to Congress. Several of them have even been elected. Therefore, I've seen not only what the liberal media will do to discredit us, but also what the treacherous Republican Party establishment is capable of as well. Like what they did to my friend Joe Miller in the 2010 U.S. Senate race in Alaska.[25]

On my show I had given a nickname to these people—Repub-licrats. The only difference between these people and Democrats is who the taxpayers' check gets written out to. The Democrats want to fill the coffers of their union buddies all in the phony name of "job creation." Republicrats prefer to line the pockets of their crony capitalist buddies and call it "economic development." But make no mistake, regardless of who the check gets written out to, both sides are running the same gangster government scam on the American taxpayer.

In my home state I saw a promising young conservative named Matt Schultz abandoned by the party establishment when he chose to take on the scion of one of the Democrat's most prominent families for Secretary of State in a bid to clean up election fraud. Being excommunicated from the Republicrat inner circle forced Schultz to actually run an aggressive, lean-and-mean, issues-based campaign. In other words, it forced him to bypass the milquetoast platitudes Republicrats normally serve up and go with the red meat that draws clearly-defined distinctions between Republicans and Democrats instead. I watched him use some of the tactics you'll be reading about later in this book.

As a result, he pulled off the biggest election night upset in my state in 2010. On the other hand, several other candidates

25 Marc Thiessen, "Jim DeMint's Courage and Lisa Murkowski's Betrayal," *Washington Post*, September 20, 2010, http://www.washingtonpost.com/wp-dyn/content/article/2010/09/20/AR2010092003019.html

embraced by the party establishment lost winnable elections. Schultz is now a rising conservative superstar you will likely hear more from nationally one day, and he doesn't owe anybody anything. I should probably mention the Democrat he defeated was one of the first hires of the new "Republican" governor of my state. I'll give the ruling class credit for one thing, they close ranks in a hurry and always have one another's backs.

As a talk show host, I make a career out of drawing clearly defined distinctions between what I believe and what I don't. As one of the most respected men in my industry once told me, *"Don't ever moderate. The best guys in this business are the ones that stay hard right and tell people what they really think."* By the grace of God, I plan on making a career out of taking that advice.

But, my show is a little different in its approach to drawing those differences. Unlike a lot of other talk shows, I don't focus exclusively on venting about the lunacy of liberalism. There is another political party that has enshrined in its platform the ideals and virtues that made these United States the most blessed and feared nation in the history of creation. That would be the Republican Party, and as long as those ideas and virtues are in its platform, then the Republican Party has a responsibility to uphold, defend, and advance them. From my perspective I don't understand the point of arguing with those that disagree with you if you can't first get those who claim to agree with you to act on your allegedly shared value system.

Therefore, from day one my radio program has been brutal on the leadership of the Republican Party. St. Peter once said "judgment begins in the house of God." Similarly, freedom, liberty, and morality in the public square begin with the political party that claims to stand for those cornerstones of our republic. Over the years it hasn't always been the social Darwinists or progressive Marxists masquerading as Keynesians who complained the most about the content of my radio program, but the Republican Party establishment.

The Republicrats have held meetings about how to get me fired. They pressured and pestered my management to get rid of me in an attempt to take food off my kids' table. They spread lies about me. They hate me because I actually think Republicans ought to stand for something other than just not being Democrats. That we ought to win elections to advance issues, otherwise there is no point to making enemies of our own friends and neighbors over politics. I ridicule Republicrats with lethal parodies. I tell the truth about their actual records. I tell my audience that the unborn child isn't any less dead because the Republicrat kills it, nor is your money any less stolen because the Republicrat took it. I help equip those who believe neither the Bible nor the Constitution are living, breathing, documents with the tools to defend and advance their belief system with both information and the right argumentation. I even take sides in primaries, giving grassroots conservatives and principled issue advocacy groups a platform to rally the masses they weren't granted access to before.

Because of this, I started having candidates or those thinking about running coming to me and asking me for advice or input on messaging and strategy. I didn't set out to do this, but there was such a void among consultants who thought it was their job to help the conservative candidate persuade voters to his principles, as opposed to consultants persuading conservative candidates to water down their principles to appease the masses, that I ended up filling this void for several folks spontaneously.

I've privately consulted with grassroots candidates on commercial scripts, speeches, and op-eds/blogs. I'm not sure how many other talk show hosts are doing things like this, and I've never been compensated for it, but I can't say no to salt-of-the-earth grassroots Americans who were fighting for the same ideals I am fighting for on the radio. Most of all, I am providing moral support for patriots who are constantly facing pressure to back down on their beliefs, and most of that pressure was coming in-house from the GOP establishment.

Speaking of the GOP establishment, when word of this eventually reached their ears they had a complete meltdown. One prominent national Republican Party figure told a friend of mine he had never seen a group of Republicans more angry and intimidated with what a local radio host was saying on the air than the Republican Party establishment was in my state with me.

Instead of being excited by an energized base they were threatened by it. They said I was hurting the party, yet when I started on the air in 2006 Democrats were on their way to total control of state government. When I left to get into national syndication in 2011, Republicans had regained the governor's mansion, attained a 60-seat majority in the statehouse, improved by five seats in the state senate, and had just defeated three State Supreme Court justices who thought they could redefine marriage in a historic retention election. Charlie Sheen called, and he thinks that's called winning. That smells like winning to me.

The establishment viewed me as the catalyst to all this new-found activism, which included the long-overdue courage to stand up to the corrupt system they had profited off of for many years. I'm not sure how much of that is true. I think in general talk show hosts fan flames much more than we spark actual fires, nonetheless I was more than happy to punch the bully in the nose and have the bully give me credit for it.

If you knew what my life was like during the Iowa Caucuses, you'd understand how I learned what you're about to read.

For example, the day of the 2011 Iowa Straw Poll I did a half dozen radio interviews around the country, spoke off the record on background to several other national reporters looking for the scoop on what was going on, hosted a nationally-syndicated radio program on the Straw Poll results, and then appeared live on Mike Huckabee's Fox News Channel television show. The week leading up to the 2012 Iowa Caucuses (which was between Christmas and New Year's, typically one of the deadest times in broadcasting) I did at least 30 radio interviews and did multiple TV hits on CNN, MSNBC, and Fox.

That's not even counting every-day occurrences like nationally-known conservatives calling me to convince me to endorse their preferred candidate, or Newt Gingrich's campaign manager calling to invite my wife and I out to dinner with the former Speaker. We ate at a sports bar (my choice), by the way, and Newt had baby-back ribs in case you were wondering (he said Callista never lets him eat like that at home).

I share this with you so that you understand where the battle-plan I am sharing with you in this book came from. Despite the fact I just turned 40 years old, have been nationally-syndicated for only two years, and before that worked in a mid-size market, I have been granted intimate access to the political process on a national scale many of the biggest names in my industry have not had the chance to see.

Drawing on that experience, I once compiled a summation of everything I've learned about politics at the request of a friend of mine running for office. When it was completed I realized that summation included 10 bullet points, so I decided to title it "Deace's 10 Commandments of Political Warfare":

1. Never trust Republicrats.
2. Never attack what you're not willing to kill.
3. Never accept the premise of your opponent's argument.
4. Never surrender the moral high ground.
5. Reverse the premise of your opponent's argument and use it against him.
6. Never, abandon your base (unless they are morally wrong).
7. Define your opponent before they define themselves & define yourself before your opponent defines you.
8. Always make your opponent defend their record and/ or their belief system.
9. Stay on message.
10. Play offense.

The past couple of years I've done several radio shows based on my 10 Commandments of Political Warfare, and to this day they remain among our most popular. I'm always flooded with emails from listeners who told me they had listened to the podcast several times after the fact, because they thought these commandments would work in their own activism at their local GOP, or even in family and neighborly discussions about politics.

Shortly after I started my nationally-syndicated program I gave a speech featuring these 10 Commandments of Political Warfare to one of the oldest Republican activist organizations in the country. Even though I was speaking between presidential candidates Ron Paul and Rick Santorum, many folks came up to me afterwards to inquire about a text version of my commandments to study and learn from.

That's when I really knew we had something special here, because these commandments can be used by every patriot reading this right now. Whether you're an elected official, running for office, an issue advocate, or just an everyday American who wants to convince their friends and neighbors why limited government undergirded by Judeo-Christian morality is the best hope for our country to preserve its prosperity, these 10 Commandments of Political Warfare can be used both on the front lines of the culture war as well as the home front.

So after seeing them work on the radio and on the campaign trail, it's now time to put them in your hands to put them to work wherever you have influence while we still have time. Benjamin Franklin once famously told a constituent who asked him what form of government he and the rest of the Founding Fathers had given us, "A republic—if you can keep it."

If we are to keep this constitutional republic, just having the right values and virtues will not be enough. We will need a plan by which to take those values and virtues with us into the arena of ideas and win, especially in a culture growing increasingly hostile to them.

The Republicans have lost the popular vote in five of the last six presidential elections because they have repeatedly violated these commandments. As you'll read in this book, the 2008 and 2012 Republican nominees, in particular, were like a case-study on what not to do if you want to win the White House. As a result, the GOP finds itself at the proverbial fork in the road.

Predictably, the party establishment that hates its own base thinks the answer is to become more like Democrats, but that is a futile pursuit. The Republican base isn't moving further left, so if the GOP establishment decides to do that it's going to need a new base (and I frankly think that's its plan). You know, for a party that is supposed to be so business smart and pragmatic you think by now they'd learn you have to serve the customers you have, not try to make your customers something they're not. Would you stop at a Burger King and expect to get an Orange Julius? So why would voters stop at the Republican Party store and expect to buy Democrat ideas? If they wanted Democrat ideas they'd go shop there.

What you will read in this book is just such a plan. But, before we discuss how we win, we must first learn why it is we lose.

1

Why We Lose

For too long conservatives have been operating under a false assumption.

This false assumption has three creeds:

1. We make up the silent majority.
2. This is still a right-of-center country.
3. Liberal media bias is primarily to blame for losing elections.

Two of these are not true, and one that is true isn't so for the reason we think it is.

It is true that this is still a right-of-center country, but we say that without recognizing the center has moved at least somewhat left. Today's moderates were liberals 40-50 years ago, when today's liberals were radicals typically relegated to seedy, dive bars listening to the Velvet Underground, or on the faculty of a college campus reading contraband copies of *Ramparts*.

Likewise, today's establishment Republican is where the mainstream of the Democrat Party used to be. So for conservatives to hang our hats on this still being a right-of-center country is like bragging about having fewer public gaffes than Joe Biden.

Furthermore, the silent majority is an antiquated term. There recently was a day when the Judeo-Christian ethic was taught and modeled quietly in the majority of our homes while the elites slouched mainly alone towards Gomorrah, but we can't even count on that anymore. We are a culture awash in moral relativism, with standards resting on shifting sands, and absolutes cast aside in favor of situational ethics. The silent majority, like the rest of America, has been Balkanized. At best nowadays, it's a silent yet substantial minority. The closest we can come now culturally to a uniform moral standard is you can do whatever you want to do as long as it doesn't hurt anybody else. In other words, everyone is wise in his own eyes.

And enough whining about liberal media bias! Is the majority of the mainstream media liberal? Umm, is the Pope Catholic? However, with the growth of alternative and social media, the percentage of the American people who use the mainstream media as their primary source of information is dwindling. It will only get smaller as more tech-savvy generations grow older. As their audience shrinks, so does their influence.

Don't forget Ronald Reagan won two landslide elections without the benefit of Fox News, Matt Drudge, or talk radio. There is so much conservative media infrastructure today that didn't exist 20-30 years ago, and some of it is among the most profitable in the industry. Our problems go way beyond messaging, which is the symptom and not the disease.

Besides, as a talk show host that's probably been interviewed for more stories by the mainstream media in the past two years than just about any of my peers (many of whom won't even talk to the mainstream media), I've also learned the *liberal* media bias we think exists is actually more of a *secular* media bias.

Many reporters, especially the ones my age and younger, have been exposed so little to Biblical teaching and Christian theology that a faith-based worldview is often just dismissed out of hand as not even worthy of their consideration. Their liberal politics is the result of a secular-progressive worldview that is often unchallenged by a Judeo-Christian moral ethic. There are times I've done interviews with these folks, and after they hear what I have to say they look at me like they're observing a new species of animal in its natural habitat. They're like, "Wow, you really exist. I only thought you were a straw man for my leftist professor(s) in college, but here you are—in the flesh."

Case in point: remember when you had the stereotypical priest coming to the rescue in the horror movie? Contemporary horror movies act as if the church doesn't even exist, and man is on his own to face evil. That is but one anecdotal example of what I'm talking about.

It is time for conservatives to stop playing the victim card, and start being honest with ourselves about where this country truly is. On my radio program we call this 3-D thinking. The first dimension is to know why you believe what you believe. The second is to know why others believe what they believe. And the third is to know why others believe what they believe about what you believe.

With that in mind, the answer as to why we've lost so much ground in this culture isn't liberal media bias, which is symptomatic of the problem. The reason we've lost so much ground in the culture is because most Americans lack the worldview our Founding Fathers had, which is the second dimension.

As far as the third dimension is concerned, most Americans do not have the proper worldview because the institutions and organizations in our culture charged with instilling it in them— primarily the family, churches, and schools—are either in societal decline or have been taken over by those who disagree with the worldview of our Founding Fathers. They are systematically purging it from these institutions and organizations as we speak.

I don't base this analysis off of my own opinions, but off of the data. I may be a man of faith but analytically I am a data-driven guy, and the data of where we are as a people is disappointing to say the least.

Worldview

According to leading worldview trend analyst George Barna,[26] only 34% of adults believe that moral truth is absolute and ethics are not situational. Just 27% of adults believe Satan is a real force of evil in the world. Didn't someone once say the devil's greatest trick was convincing mankind he doesn't exist? That appears to have worked on about three-fourths of the American people, and 72% of them also believe they can earn their way to Heaven by being good (and of course the standard for good is highly subjective) rejecting the traditional Christian notion that it is by the death and resurrection of Jesus Christ (you know, the Easter story) we are reconciled with our Creator.

Add this all up, and Barna concludes that since he started surveying American belief systems in 1995, the percentage of adults with the same basic Judeo-Christian worldview as our Founding Fathers has typically ranged from 7-9%. Yet at the same time 83% of Americans consider themselves to be Christians. Go figure.

A worldview isn't the same as a moralview. Most Americans still possess on some level a basic Judeo-Christian moralview, even if it's polluted in certain places by contemporary influences like moral relativism and situational ethics.

I would define a Judeo-Christian moralview as rightly knowing where right and wrong comes from, and who the ultimate determiner of right and wrong is. A Judeo-Christian worldview is rightly integrating that knowledge of right and wrong, and who we're ultimately accountable to, into our daily lives so that it becomes the main influence for the decisions and choices we make. In other words, actions speak louder than words.

For example, you're supporting a truly principled conservative against a Republicrat hack in a primary. Your guy loses said primary,

---

26 "Barna Survey Examines Changes in Worldviews Among Christians Over the Past 13 Years," Barna Research Group, March 6, 2009, https://www.barna.org/barna-update/article/21-transformation/252-barna-survey-examines-changes-in-worldview-among-christians-over-the-past-13-years#.UlxBG1AjJXY

and now the GOP establishment begins its sanctimonious (and fingernails on a chalkboard annoying) calls to coalesce because the Democrat is allegedly so much worse (when in many cases they turn out to be one in the same). You dig in your heels and say no way, you've read this book before and every time you swallow your integrity and vote for the Republicrat, he/she then makes you regret it nearly every day they're in office. You're bound and determined you won't fall for the banana in the tailpipe anymore.

But then the Republicrat goes head-to-head with the Democrat, and you notice that by comparison he's articulating a viewpoint so much closer to your own. In fact, he's starting to sound so good that now you're wondering why you raised such a stink in the primary in the first place? You start questioning yourself, and wondering if the Republican Party establishment has been right about conservatives all along, we are impossible to please. Dag gum, if you knew all along this guy was so good, you would've urged others to coalesce sooner to keep your powder dry for the general.

You relent, and it's once more unto the breach for you. You're now all in for the Republicrat to beat the Democrat you believe is the clear and present danger. You're excited that your guy ends up winning on election night, and you're at the victory party. Sure, you feel a little uneasy because you're hanging out with all the people that keep giving you excuses as to why they can't do what you elected them to do, but you believe in grace and redemption. Who knows, maybe they've seen the light and are finally listening to conservatives like you?

However, it doesn't take long after they're sworn in for the principled rhetoric to cease and the same-old, same-old to resume. Meet the new boss, same as the old boss. Now you're just months into the Republicrat's milquetoast reign of lukewarm spit and already you're kicking yourself wondering why you fell for the banana in the tailpipe yet again. Especially because this time you were so sure your guy was showing real moral conviction on the campaign trail.

So what happened?

What happened was your friendly neighborhood Republicrat has a superior moralview to his Democrat opponent (or does a good job of convincing you he does), and when the moralview of the establishment Republican and the liberal Democrat were compared side-by-side the establishment Republican's—while not exactly ideal—was clearly superior. However, once in office the Republicrat's moralview never transitions into a worldview, so he is either unwilling or incapable of integrating his moralview into his governing. Instead, his moralview becomes subjected to the whims of polls and avoiding conflict at all costs with those terrifying and intimidating liberal pundits who might say mean things about him.

His moralview gives him the right *positions*, but it's his worldview that gives him the right *convictions*. Positions are negotiable based on pressures and perceptions. Convictions are non-negotiable absolutes driven by an internal confidence that your cause is just, thus being criticized by the very people you're trying to defeat is a sign to you that you're on the right path. Without a proper understanding of one's place in the world, and whom one is ultimately accountable to for their actions and choices while a part of it, one cannot have the right worldview. And it's only with the right worldview that one acquires the correct courage of conviction.

A politician has positions. A statesman has convictions, and pledges his life, fortune, and sacred honor to defend and advance them. Unfortunately, the other side has more statesmen of (albeit wrong) conviction than we do.

They would rather shut down the government than stop funding the child killers at Planned Parenthood with taxpayer dollars. Our side responds by extending the debt ceiling to avoid a government shutdown, thus filling Planned Parenthood's coffers with the taxpayer's money once more. They lose 32 consecutive elections on the definition of marriage, and their leaders keep coming back for more. We win 32 consecutive elections on marriage, and our "leaders" want to run away and hide from the issue—or start a Super Pac to support destroying marriage.[27]

Although it's misplaced and morally flawed, the Left is

---

27 Maggie Haberman, "Pro-Gay Rights Super PAC Backs 3 GOPers," *Politico*, August 16, 2012, http://www.politico.com/news/stories/0812/79774.html

demonstrating more courage of conviction than we are. And as long as that is the case, we're going to keep losing ground in the culture as well as at the polls.

Taxes and Spending

Most Americans instinctively know the growth of government is out of control, but when you look at the real numbers it's even worse than most of us realize.[28]

In 1980 the federal government collected $244,069 billion from individual taxpayers. Just 30 years later, in 2010, that number climbed to just over $2.3 trillion. Keep in mind this is only *individual* income taxes, and doesn't count Social Security, capital gains, or other taxes like excise taxes, which are applied to things such as gasoline, firearms and other weapons, tobacco, alcohol, tires, trucks, and fishing equipment. King George III had nothing on Washington, D.C.

The $700 billion increase in the federal budget under President George W. Bush was far and away the biggest in American history at the time, until Barack Obama's spending spree. Despite the fact none of Obama's proposed bloated budgets have made it into law (the Democrats didn't even vote for them when they were in the majority), the deficit has reached 100% of our gross domestic product, which is the total market value of a nation's combined goods and services. We have become, in every sense of the term, a debtor nation.

Life

Did you know the income for Planned Parenthood, America's top infanticide merchant, increased by 24% and its government subsidies have grown by 33% since 2005 alone? More revenue has allowed Planned Parenthood to get even more gruesomely

---

28 Steve Deace and Gregg Jackson, "Introduction," *We Won't Get Fooled Again: Where the Christian Right Went Wrong and How to Make America Right Again,* (Denver: J&J Publishing, 2011), 18-20.

innovative in its brutality. After the slaughter of over 50 million children, life is so disregarded now that child killing via abortion is available via teleconference. A 2011 Rasmussen Poll[29] found that most Americans considered themselves "pro-choice" (in favor of killing children) but also found abortion immoral in most circumstances. That's some real moral confusion right there.

Family

According to a 2010 study,[30] the out-of-wedlock birth rate in the United States has skyrocketed from 28% in 1990 to an incredible 41% today. The out-of-wedlock birthrate 30 years ago was 19.6%. Translation: despite much more awareness, acceptance, and access to birth control, as well as millions of taxpayer dollars invested in abstinence programs, more and more children in this country are conceived by parents who are not married.

The current divorce rate in America for first time marriages is 41%. For second marriages it's 60%, and for third marriages it's 73%. While divorce rates did decline from 1981-90, for the first time in American history a couple is just as likely to be parted by divorce on average as by death. Also for the first time in American history, married couples are the minority with the majority of American adults either living together or remaining single.

Education

Education is the second biggest industry behind energy in America, and it's one of the largest total expenditures for government at all

---

29 Steven Ertfelt, "Majority Say Abortion Morally Wrong, But Call Themselves Pro-Choice," *Life News,* May 26, 2011, http://www.lifenews.com/2011/05/26/majority-say-abortion-morally-wrong-but-call-themselves-pro-choice/

30 Steve Deace and Gregg Jackson, "Introduction," *We Won't Get Fooled Again: Where the Christian Right Went Wrong and How to Make America Right Again,* (Denver: J&J Publishing, 2011), 21-23.

levels as well. Nonetheless, the government education system in America, as depicted by must-see films like *Waiting for Superman*, is a pandemic of failure. Much of the hand-wringing is over American students' paltry proficiency in math and science, but the real concern again comes down to worldview.

A recent Department of Education survey[31] found history is the weakest subject among American students. Only 20 percent of 6th graders, 17 percent of 8th graders, and 12 percent of high school seniors demonstrate a solid grasp on their nation's history, which means they grow increasingly ignorant the longer they're in school. A majority of 4th graders didn't know why Abraham Lincoln was important. Nearly 80 percent of 12th graders incorrectly identified North Korea's ally against the U.S. in the Korean War, despite the fact it was a multiple choice question.

In 2011 *Newsweek* administered the U.S. citizenship test[32] to 1,000 American citizens, and the results were tragic. Here are just a few examples:

- 33% of Americans could not identify when the *Declaration of Independence* was signed.
- 65% of Americans couldn't say what happened at the Constitutional Convention.
- 80% of Americans didn't know who was president during World War I.

In 2012, Xavier University did its own national poll of Americans using[33] ten questions from the U.S. citizenship test. Only one in three Americans correctly answered at least six of the

---

31 Jeff Jacoby, "Don't Know Much About History," *The Boston Globe,* June 19, 2011, http://www.boston.com/bostonglobe/editorial_opinion/oped/articles/2011/06/19/dont_know_much_about_history/

32 "Take the Quiz: What Do We Know?" *Newsweek,* March 20, 2011, http://mag.newsweek.com/2011/03/20/take-the-quiz-what-we-don-t-know.html

33 Gregory Korte, "Americans Put to Shame by Immigrants on Sample Civics Test," *USA Today,* April 27, 2012, http://usatoday30.usatoday.com/news/nation/story/2012-04-26/imiigrant-civics-test-americans-fail/54563612/1

questions, which is required for a passing score. The results go downhill from there:

- 59% of Americans could not name one enumerated power of the federal government found in the U.S. Constitution.
- 62% of Americans could not name the governor of their state.
- 85% of Americans did not know the meaning of "the rule of law."
- 75% of Americans could not answer the question "what does the judiciary branch do?"
- 71% of Americans were unable to identify the Constitution as the "supreme law of the land."
- 62% of Americans could not name at least one of their two U.S. Senators.
- 62% of Americans could not name the Speaker of the House.

Can you say low-information voter? As if all this data weren't depressing enough, in 2011 the Intercollegiate Studies Institute surveyed 165 Americans who have been elected to public office. Here are some of its findings:[34]

- Only 49% could name all three branches of government.
- Only 46% knew that Congress, not the president, has the power to declare war.
- Only 15% knew the phrase "separation of church and state" never appears in the U.S. Constitution.
- Only 57% knew what the Electoral College was, and 20% of those that didn't thought that it was a school for "training those aspiring for higher political office."

In other words, our politicians are even more ignorant about whom we are and how we're supposed to govern ourselves than

---

34 http://www.americancivicliteracy.org/ (2011)

the American people are. The dumber we become, the bigger the government gets because we can't have self-government if we don't know what the government is supposed to do. How can we possibly expect to successfully defend America's traditions and ideals when most Americans don't even know what they are?

I'm reminded of a private roundtable with former Speaker Newt Gingrich I once sat in on, and Gingrich made the observation we're never going to decentralize power from the beltway and empower self-government again until the American people become much more informed and much more involved.

If freedom and liberty are always just a generation away from being lost, then it appears in the last generation we've completely lost our moral compass that makes freedom and liberty possible in the first place, which means we've got a generation to recover before we cease being citizens and start being subjects.

A lot of you reading this already possess that sense of urgency, as the mounting Republicrat casualties in primaries nationwide prove. We're spurred to action, but now we need to channel that sense of urgency and courage of conviction into something sustainable and constructive over the long-term. Lots of books, blogs, and talk radio programs are done by conservatives each day discussing *what* needs to be done, *why* it needs to be done, and *who* needs to do it. Unfortunately, there's very little done on *how* to do it.

Until now.

2

Never Trust Republicrats

Re-pub-li-crat noun, plural **Republicrats:** *Segment of the American ruling class pretending to be conservatives by paying lip service to conservative principles, and camouflaging themselves in patriotic imagery. Often confused with RINOs (Republicans in Name Only), but Republicrats are far more dangerous because they've learned how to campaign on conservative talking points. Unlike the RINO who campaigns and governs from the middle-left, the Republicrat campaigns as a conservative and then governs middle-left. Once in office the record of the Republicrat is virtually indistinguishable from the Democrats regardless of the rhetoric, either because of cowardice, deception, or a combination of both.*

Cicero, one of ancient Rome's most famous orators and philosophers, might as well have been talking about Republicrats when he said:

A nation can survive its fools, and even the ambitious. But it cannot survive treason from within. An enemy at the gates is less formidable, for he is known and carries his banner openly. But the traitor moves amongst those within the gate freely, his sly whispers rustling through all the alleys, heard in the very halls of government itself. For the traitor appears not a traitor; he speaks in accents familiar to his victims, and he wears their face and their arguments, he appeals to the baseness that lies deep in the hearts of all men. He rots the soul of a nation (or movement), he works secretly and unknown in the night to undermine the pillars of the city, he infects the body politic so that it can no longer resist. A murderer is less to fear.

Conservatives have spent decades fighting to purge RINOs (Republicans in Name Only) from the Republican Party, but it turns out the Arlen Specters of the world were little more than a diversion. To a lesser extent the same could be said of the Left. While it is true they would love nothing more than to shred whatever is left of our beloved Constitution and transform our republic into a Western European-style socialist mobocracy, they cannot do it alone. Culprits always need collaborators. Especially when they hold minority views in a majority rules country:

- Twice as many Americans describe themselves as ideologically conservative rather than liberal.[35]
- Three times more Americans believe in some variant of the Biblical account of creation[36] as the origin of the human species than do atheistic evolution (humans evolved from natural means alone).

---

35 Lydia Saad, "Conservatives Remain Largest Ideological Group," Gallup Polling, January 12, 2012, http://www.gallup.com/poll/152021/conservatives-remain-largest-ideological-group.aspx

36 Frank Newport, "In U.S., 46% Hold Creationist View of Human Origins," Gallup Polling, June 1, 2012, http://www.gallup.com/poll/155003/hold-creationist-view-human-origins.aspx

- Less than 2% of the American population identifies themselves as homosexual.[37]
- 74% of Americans want the government to cut deficits, only 8% of Americans want tax increases[38] to be the focus of deficit reduction, and a majority of Americans favor scrapping the federal income tax.
- 75% of Americans oppose funding the killing of children (abortion) with taxpayer dollars.[39]

I could continue citing public opinion data that is similarly favorable to conservatives on a wide swath of issues, but by now you get the picture. Yet despite widespread public approval for many basic conservative principles, the statists still maintain widespread control of the government schools, the ruling class routinely caves to the moral depravity lobby, the government continues to grow regardless of who's in power, and the child killers at Planned Parenthood continue to pick the taxpayers' pocket.

To understand why this is the case, you must first understand the three primary languages used in contemporary American politics.

The first—and sadly least spoken—is plain English, which is the language spoken by those of us that actually believe the original wording of the Constitution means exactly what it says. Unfortunately, without cultural revival coming soon this commonsense form of expression could become a dead language.

The second—and sadly most spoken—is political correctness. This Orwellian double-speak introduces self-contradictory terms

---

37 Garance Franke-Ruta, "Americans Have No Idea How Few Gay People There Really Are," *The Atlantic*, May 31, 2012, http://www.theatlantic.com/politics/archive/2012/05/americans-have-no-idea-how-few-gay-people-there-are/257753/

38 Meredith Bragg and Nick Gillespie, "Reason-Rupe Poll: 96% Worried About Federal Debt, 74% Want Spending Cap," Reason.com, May 3, 2011, http://reason.com/archives/2011/05/03/reason-rupe-poll-96-worry-abou

39 Yates Walker, "The Next Big Scandal: Taxpayer-Funded Abortion," *Daily Caller*, March 13, 2012, http://dailycaller.com/2012/03/13/the-next-big-scandal-taxpayer-funding-for-abortion/

like "marriage equality" (when any guy that's been married for more than six months can tell you no such thing exists) and "reproductive freedom" (which doesn't make sense since you're killing your reproduction anyway, so why would you want the freedom to reproduce in the first place).

This language takes commonly used words and phrases and strips all common sense from them, thus changing their long-standing and previously acknowledged meaning. For example, "tolerance" used to mean I put up with you even if I disagree with you because it's a free country. Nowadays under political correctness, "tolerance" means you lose your freedom if you don't validate and participate in everything I do that you don't approve of.

The third is a technocratic dialect used only by the Republicrat ruling class, and is meant to throw grassroots conservative patriots off the scent before they realize the Republicans they're supporting are doing practically nothing they were sent there to do. It attempts to convince conservatives that their elected representatives believe in the same plain English they do. However, the group communicating the message means something totally different than those receiving it think/hope they do, so the mind-numbing clichés intentionally get lost in translation. Republicrat lingo is sometimes also referred to as "gibberish," "jargon," or the crass description for the byproduct of a bull's bowel movement.

I have spent years observing Republicrats in their natural habitat in an earnest attempt to make sense of this foul beast wreaking havoc on humanity—and the U.S. Constitution. After much careful study, I believe I finally discovered the Republicrat Rosetta Stone, and have cracked their confusing code of complete crap.

What I found is there are ten phrases used most often by Republicrats. If we can decipher the true meaning of these ten phrases, unlocking the rest of their sinister secrets instantly becomes much easier.

10. "Something must be done." = Better to violate our oath of office and betray our base now rather than risk the wrath of the liberal media later.

Most of the worst ideas in human history began with cries that "something must be done." But when Republicrats utter that phrase, that is a tell they're about to do exactly what the progressive/Marxist/Leftists want to do, they just need to conjure up a phony crisis in order to justify it.

9. "Reagan couldn't get nominated today." = Thank goodness conservatives don't have a real leader like that nowadays to expose our scam.

This is a whiny lament frequently utilized by those who either hated Ronald Reagan back in the day, or put up with him because he was a winner. Even before he left office, many of these same people systematically went about undoing his legacy in order to maintain their corporatist gravy train. Now that Reagan isn't around to speak for himself, and given the fact conservatives lack leaders with his considerable skills, these political hacks use this line every time conservatives demand Republicans act like Republicans and not Democrats.

8. "Leadership." = Surrender to Democrats and liberal media now before it's too late.

The Republicrat's primary motivation is to avoid the searing pain of being called nasty names by the liberal media, or not being described as "reasonable" by their Democrat colleagues. So while they use all of our attack words on camera or in press releases, that's really just a signal to the American Left they're ready to negotiate the terms of surrender once they've patronized their base with the talking points that gives them the warm fuzzy.

7. "We need to focus on jobs." = Thank goodness the economy sucks so we have an excuse for standing for nothing.

Please note, this self-explanatory Republicrat mantra is only used when Democrats are in power in any branch of government, and does not apply when the Republicans are. When Republicans are in power, substitute any reference to socialism or Jimmy Carter as the appropriate scare tactic for that situation.

6. "Team player." = Somebody who cares more about being liked, getting their ego stroked, advancing their own ambitions, and/or getting a seat at our very wobbly table than taking a righteous stand.

The prime directive of the Republicrat Machine is to begat more Republicrats in order to perpetuate their taxpayer-funded fraud. If someone isn't a team player, it's because that person actually got into politics to govern on a set of conservative principles and they stubbornly insist on sticking to those principles. Therefore, their very existence threatens to expose the entire Republicrat charade. The Republicrats will typically punish such would-be statesmen by excommunicating said non-team player from all Republicrat functions, and cutting off his access to the campaign purse strings. Better for one principled patriot to die then for their entire scam to perish.

5. "Big Tent." = Marginalize conservatives to avoid exposing the fact we're actually embarrassed by the Republican Party platform.

Despite all the strategic talk of winning elections, the real reason Republicrats seek to bring in those who don't really believe in small government and Judeo-Christian morality is to dilute the influence within the party of those that do.

4. "Democrats weren't going to budge." = We either don't care about your moral convictions or don't share them. Either way, thank the God we constantly patronize with our contrived talking points we've still got the Democrats around to shift the blame to when we just really want to go home, or living up to our campaign promises to shrink government and defund Planned Parenthood is just too dang hard.

There are only two possible reasons why the two shortest books ever written are "French War Heroes" and "Republicans Who Actually Have a Spine." One, Republicrats all attended the Neville

Chamberlain School of Realpolitik. Two, they want the kind of government the Democrats want, but want to be able to blame it on the Democrats when we get it. We'll let Occam's razor determine which one it is.

3. "Incrementalism." = Giving the Democrats 80% of what they want and then bragging half a loaf is better than none.

Republicrats claim victory by going over the pagan progressive cliff the American Left has put us on a collision course with a little slower than the Democrats would prefer. Republicrats put cultural oblivion on cruise control, while the Democrats put the pedal to the medal. That's Republicrat incrementalism—a slower, more tortuous death.

2. "Bi-partisan." = There's just enough pork in this unconstitutional crap sandwich to justify voting for it.

See TARP and way too much of the George W. Bush presidency for recent examples.

1. "Coalesce." = Unite now to lose to Democrats even sooner.

Republicrats usually call for coalescing around their candidate within minutes of his official campaign announcement, long before a single primary vote is cast. In Republicrat world, primaries are bad because they expose their cockroaches to sunlight, thus making it tougher for the party to come together later on in the general election once grassroots conservative patriots get a good and sickening glimpse at the pile of dung they'll have to plug their noses to vote for. You know, like Mitch McConnell.[40]

For example, should a conservative win a presidential primary or caucus, Republicrats will respond by escalating their frantic calls to "coalesce" lest we risk wasting resources when the Democrats are obviously so much worse. I believe Republicrats started calling for the party to coalesce in time for 2016 approximately

---

40 Jack Brammer, "Campaign Manager on Working for Mitch McConnell: 'Holding My Nose'," *Lexington Herald-Leader*, August 8, 2013, http://www.kentucky .com/2013/08/08/2756443/campaign-manager-on-working-for.html

six seconds after Romney lost in 2012. It doesn't matter they don't have a candidate yet. If it was up to the Republicrats, they would just run a candidate named "coalesce."

I'm a big sports fan. Although football is my favorite sport, my favorite sporting event is the NCAA Men's Basketball Tournament. I even love the lead up to March Madness, and all the speculation about which teams will and won't get invited.

One of the things ESPN does each year at that time is a blind NCAA Tournament resume comparison between two teams, so viewers get a chance to see the objective merits of each team without being prejudiced by the power of the brand (or lack thereof). Almost always in these comparisons the team with the stronger resume is from a smaller conference, compared to the name team from the power conference.

Let's do the same thing with American presidents.

Here is the profile for "A": Signed into law the most extensive overhaul and strictest reform of the welfare system, was the last president to sign into law a balanced budget, and signed the Defense of Marriage Act into law that defined marriage between one man and one woman.

Here is the profile for "B": Oversaw the biggest expansion of the federal budget and the size of government ever at that point in American history, signed into law the biggest single welfare program in American history prior to Obamacare, and signed into law the biggest federal intervention into education since the creation of the Department of Education in the 1970s.

Without knowing who either A or B is, just about every grassroots conservative patriot would prefer A to B, right? But what if I told you that "A" represents Democrat Bill Clinton, and "B" represents Republican George W. Bush?

In fact, I could make a strong case George W. Bush's lasting legacy will do more damage to the conservative movement than the Left could've ever dreamed. In addition to his record I've already referred to, there's his appointment of John Roberts as the Chief Justice of the United States Supreme Court. In one week in June of 2012, Roberts was the tie-breaking vote on court opinions that said a sovereign state (in this case Arizona) cannot enforce the U.S. Constitution without explicit consent from the federal government, and if the feds won't enforce the Constitution the states still can't do it and have to pick up the tab for lawlessness nevertheless.

Then Roberts was the deciding vote on upholding Obamacare, when he essentially said the federal government can do whatever it wants to you provided government's perceived need is great enough; which means there are *no* limits to federal government power. Perhaps the feds "need" to impose martial law to silence all those Tea Partiers on the homeland security watch list?

According to Bush's own judicial appointee, the feds can do whatever they want since the Constitution is based on "need" and not "law," which means we really have no Constitution at all since its original intent was to limit the size and scope of government power—not individual liberty.

Just like it was Republican judicial appointees for the U.S. Supreme Court that gave us *Roe v. Wade*, *Kelo v. New London*, *Lawrence v. Texas*, and most of the other worst and most unconstitutional court rulings in recent American history.

So the next time some Republicrat political hack sanctimoniously tries to tell you that you have to vote for the Republicrat to get conservative judges do yourself and America a favor. Slap on a pair of steel-toed boots, kick that son of a gun in the shins as hard as you can, and dedicate that comeuppance to John Roberts while you're at it.

Don't get me wrong, I'm not making the case to support Bill Clinton over George W. Bush, although we actually got smaller government under Bubba. Let's remember that Clinton's first term went hard left with Hillarycare, the Brady Bill, and one of the largest tax increases in American history.

Clinton ran in 1992 as "a new Democrat," except that once in office his administration looked like the old "New Deal." The result was the historic repudiation Clinton received via the 1994 midterm elections, which vaulted the Republicans into control of Congress for the first time in decades. All of the positives from the

Clinton years I referenced occurred *after* Republicans gained control of Congress, and started dragging Clinton to the right.

In fact, the final phase of the Clinton Administration, combined with Republicans controlling Congress, produced perhaps the most conservative term for an American president since Calvin Coolidge or Reagan's first term.

George W. Bush had the luxury of a Republican-controlled House of Representatives for six years of his presidency, and a GOP-controlled Senate for four years. Yet he governed to the left of Clinton with a Republican Congress.

There are two reasons for this.

First, Republican leaders in Congress held the line against a Democrat president, but then decided to be "team players" once their big government guy got in the White House. In other words, honoring the group-think meant more than honoring their sworn oaths of office.

Second, George W. Bush wasn't a conservative. Sure, he was more conservative than John Kerry or Al Gore, but being *more* conservative than someone is not the same as being *a* conservative. I may look better in a Speedo than Chris Christie, but that doesn't mean that anybody actually wants to see me in one.

It's easy to blame architect Karl Rove, the wannabe Svengali of the GOP, for the cynical realpolitik of "compassionate conservatism." But as Morton Blackwell at the Leadership Institute has said for years, "Personnel is policy."

A conservative doesn't hire a soul-less technocrat like Rove to put lipstick on a pig, because they're going to look for advisors that help them reach the American people with their principles. Republicrats have to hire consultants like Rove, who are fluent in their empty technocratic dialect.

Republicrats like Rove, and the generation of bratty technocrats he's currently spawning within the GOP, believe you win to lead. Those of us in the grassroots believe you lead to win, and there is a difference.

If you begin with the premise you win to lead, then you base your campaign on the technique or craftsmanship of the messaging (i.e. fundraising, polls, focus groups, talking points, etc.) rather than the merits of the message. This brings us to my definition of a technocrat: someone who is only or primarily concerned with the political process itself and not the principles at stake. To paraphrase former NBA all-star Allen Iverson, "We talking about process, man. Not the principles . . . not the principles, but the process." All technocrats talk and care about is the process.

It's not that the techniques and the craftsmanship (process) aren't important, but these aren't student body elections we're talking about here. This is the real world, and we're electing politicians who make life-or-death, prosperity-or-poverty decisions daily. Without a solid moral basis for these decisions, we end up on shifting sands at best or a ditch at worst.

Conservatives believe you lead to win, otherwise what's the point of winning if it's not actually to do something once we get there? The overwhelming victory of Wisconsin Governor Scott Walker in his 2012 recall election is an excellent example of this. Walker stood firm on principle in a traditionally blue state and got more votes in his recall election than he got when he originally won the office.

Standing for conservative principles unites conservatives. People like me all over the country that detest the Republican Party establishment, and their milquetoast presidential candidates, were strongly united behind Walker. Why? Because he gave us something to vote *for* and not just *against*. With his base united, Walker was free to play offense and try to pick off soft Democrat voters, and according to Fox News' exit polling he got 18% of the Obama voters in his recall.[41]

A united and enthusiastic base plus almost one-fifth of your opponent's voters equals blowout, and that's just what Walker got. Blowout equals mandate, and Walker got one of those as well. Now it's up to Walker to honor that mandate, and if he does he can be President of these United States one day if he wants to be.

---

41 "Exit Poll: Tea Party Key to Walker's Win," Fox News, June 5, 2012, http://nation. foxnews.com/scott-walker/2012/06/06/exit-poll-tea-party-key-walker-win

Contrast Walker's booming with Tim Pawlenty's bust. Pawlenty was also elected governor of a traditionally blue state, and did some good things—though none of them near as bold as Walker taking on the government sector employee unions that are at the core of the Democrat power base. After serving two terms as Minnesota governor Pawlenty ran for president. Despite spending more money leading up to the crucial Iowa Straw Poll than any of his fellow competitors, and the fact Iowa is a neighboring state he visited enough to qualify for residency, Pawlenty was out of the race five months before the actual Iowa Caucuses because of a poor showing in the Iowa Straw Poll.

Perhaps it's because folks saw Pawlenty as a hack, and they see Walker as a leader. Remember when Pawlenty labeled Romneycare as "Obamneycare" in an interview during the 2012 Republican presidential primary cycle, and then in a debate the very next day cowardly declined to confront Romney directly when he had the chance?

Three days prior to the Iowa Straw Poll, Pawlenty looked me right in the eye and told me, "I'm running so that someone like Romney doesn't become our nominee." He even took documentation of Romney's appalling record appointing judges in Massachusetts (22 of the 36 judges Governor Romney appointed were Democrats)[42] that I shared with him and brought it up at the pre-Straw Poll presidential debate 24 hours later. A month later, Pawlenty endorsed Romney for president.

Pawlenty isn't a RINO, he's a Republicrat. A RINO runs as pro-child killing, and governs that way. A RINO runs as big government, and stays that way. A RINO runs as anti-family and pro-immorality, and stays that way. A Republicrat runs as a conservative, and may even do some conservative things when it's easy. But when push comes to shove a Republicrat puts his own comfort ahead of his country.

RINOs are almost always native to traditional blue states, so

---

42 Brian Moony, "Taking Office, Remaining an Outsider," *The Boston Globe*, June 29, 2007, http://www.boston.com/news/politics/2008/specials/romney/articles/part6_main/?page=full

they're easily identifiable. Republicrats are more versatile, which makes them more dangerous and more prevalent. Since they offer no real threat to the liberal power structure they can win in blue states, and since they know what conservatives want to hear they can win in red states. Former Congressman J.C. Watts once told me conservatives are in danger of devolving from a movement to an industry, and the closer we come to that happening the more Republicrats will roll off the assembly line of the machine.

Republicrats are a cancer that is metastasizing and eating away at the conservative movement, and taking the country down with them. They act as human shields between us and the statists, because when we take a stand it reveals their own cowardice and duplicity.

Don't waste time wondering what the motivation for their treachery is, because whether it's gutlessness or corruption the end game is the same. Any good pastor will tell you part of his job is to feed sheep and shoot wolves. Sheep are some of the most naïve creatures on the planet, and will walk right into a slaughter if they don't have a shepherd. They are in need of constant care, discipling, mercy, and tending.

Wolves, however, are pure predators. When wolves are allowed among the sheep they devour the sheep. The most dangerous wolves of them all are the ones in sheep's clothing, or the "treason within" Cicero once described.

All of us, including our politicians, make mistakes as either sheep or wolves.

Some of our elected officials are decent public servants who just make mistakes because nobody's perfect. They would be sheep. You can tell if they're sheep because they either don't know any better, or when confronted with the right path they acknowledge they were on the wrong one.

For example, during the 2012 presidential cycle I was impressed with the way Newt Gingrich was willing to speak openly and be held accountable for his past adultery and failed marriages. Whenever it came up on the Iowa Caucus campaign trail I never once saw him try to avoid the subject, or act like there were bigger things to talk about in the campaign. He even did an interview on my show the week before the 2012 Iowa Caucuses with Donald Wildmon of the American Family Association addressing the topic once more.

I met several of his family members who were willing to vouch for the positive changes in his life (I am always suspicious of men trying to sell you on them as a leader when their own families aren't around, and don't seem publicly invested in what they're doing, because these are the people that know him best). I also talked to people like Pastor Jim Garlow in San Diego, who had spent some time personally discipling Gingrich in recent years.

However, a wolf not only doesn't know the right path, he doesn't want to know. A wolf has no intention of being anything other than a wolf. Sure, for a time he might dress up like grandma to fool Little Red Riding Hood, but sooner or later the claws come out.

An example of this would be Mitt Romney. People have asked me for years why I'm so hard on his past betrayals of conservative orthodoxy when Ronald Reagan was once pro-child killing and gave us no-fault divorce. The difference is Reagan openly discussed his mistakes and failures, and didn't try to cover them up. In fact, Reagan once said the greatest regret of his political career was signing the first no-fault divorce law in America. Another sign of true repentance is when someone feels the responsibility to act on their newfound conviction and make up for past mistakes. Reagan wrote the powerful book *Abortion and the Conscience of a Nation* to defend the moral conviction he once opposed, and was the originator of the so-called "Mexico City Policy" that prohibited the U.S. Government from exporting child-killing beyond our shores.

This humility and transparency from Reagan inspires integrity in others. I'm not saying Reagan was a saint, because he wasn't. He was just a man. A good man doesn't have to be perfect, but he does have to be consistent. Meaning over the long haul of his life you may see ups and downs, but overall you see long obedience in the right direction. Unfortunately, supporting Romney costs others their credibility. To this day Romney remains unrepentant as he flip-flops with impunity, and continues to lie and distort his liberal record as governor of Massachusetts. Like signing Romney-care and its taxpayer-funded abortions for just $50 per kill (free for low-income women) into law *after* his alleged pro-life conversion. Like failing to sign the Susan B. Anthony or Personhood USA pro-life pledges during the 2012 presidential campaign.

And like a bad rash Romney keeps coming back. Like Michael Myers or Jason Voorhees in a cheesy '80s slasher flick he cannot be stopped. Like the character Milton Waddams in the '90s cult classic *Office Space* he refuses to accept his firing.

Romney is Rasputin.

They fed Rasputin wine and cakes laced with cyanide and that didn't work. They shot Rasputin and that didn't work. They beat him to a pulp, even removing his penis according to legend, and that didn't work. They couldn't get rid of him until they bound his body and threw him in an icy river.

By no means am I suggesting we treat Romney the same way. I'm simply suggesting that some people just can't seem to take a hint. You'd think that after you were rejected despite spending five years and a sizable chunk of your (and others) fortune to win the presidency—not to mention taking every side of each issue—you might come to the conclusion you're not wanted. Especially given how quickly your base was willing to move on to the future the nanosecond after you lost. But some mosquitoes refuse to be swatted away.

The GOP establishment's latest master plan that back-fired reemerged after his election loss to "assert himself as a party elder,"[43] whatever the Sam Hill that means. Normally elders are men of vision, wisdom, consistency, and substance.

Since Romney is none of those things[44] he apparently fits right in as an elder in today's dazed and confused Republican Party.[45]

---

43 Michael O'Brien, "Romney Re-Enters GOP Fray," NBC News, August 7, 2013, http://firstread.nbcnews.com/_news/2013/08/07/19914511-romney-re-enters-gop-fray?lite

44 Steve Baldwin, "The Case Against Mitt Romney," January 23, 2012, http://stevedeace.com/news/iowa-politics/the-case-against-mitt-romney/

45 Steve Deace, "Undocumented Democrats," *Townhall*, August 10, 2013, http://townhall.com/columnists/stevedeace/2013/08/10/undocumented-democrats-n1658738

See, in today's Republican Party the loser gets the spoils. Jimmy Carter may gallivant around the globe as an international man of mystery, but he's not been considered a serious player in Democrat Party politics since the embarrassment that was his presidency. Keep in mind that unlike Romney, Carter actually won the White House against an embattled incumbent president. Romney—ironically enough—finished with 47%.

Why anybody would take seriously a man who is only the third person in American history to lose to a president who actually lost support from his previous election is beyond me. It would be like today's young NFL quarterbacks taking advice on how to win the Super Bowl from Tony Romo instead of Tom Brady.

But there were rising GOP "stars" Chris Christie, Paul Ryan, and Rand Paul lining up to be feted at a Romney retreat in 2013. And there was Romney urging Republicans not to defund Obamacare, which don't forget was actually Romney's horrible idea before Obama's. Instead, Romney urged the Republican Party to "rally around electable candidates."[46]

You can't make this stuff up.

Dan Balz of *The Washington Post* came on my show once to discuss his book *Collision 2012* about the 2012 presidential election, which was really a book about every election the Republicans have lost since 1976. The names just change to protect the not-so-innocent.

In the book, Balz said the Romney family took a poll about dad running for president in 2012 and Willard himself wasn't in favor of running. Romney didn't want to run, but now he just can't stay away. Romney has now officially flip-flopped on everything.

A man that wants to portray himself as a reluctant warrior has become a zit that won't pop. And he's not alone. Whether it's Bob Dole or John "little ball of hate" McCain, several past GOP nominees

---

46 Peter Grier, "Mitt Romney to GOP: Don't Shutdown Government to Kill Obamacare," *Christian Science Monitor,* August 7, 2013, http://www.csmonitor.com/USA/DC-Decoder/Decoder-Wire/2013/0807/Mitt-Romney-to-GOP-Don-t-shut-down-government-to-kill-Obamacare

have come out of the woodwork to provide their unsolicited un-sage advice on why the GOP has lost the popular vote in 5 of the last 6 presidential elections. And what do Romney, McCain, and Dole have in common? They're all losers. They're all men a majority of the American people rejected when they had the chance to select them as commander-in-chief. So here's a simple question: if the "advice" these guys are giving is so good then why didn't they win?

Anybody?

Anybody?

Of course, nobody in the mainstream media will ask such a question because these are the standard-bearers for the Republican Party they want—lovable losers. Not to mention the party establishment each of these men represents and the mainstream media have a common foe.

Us.

Sadly there have been some once-respected conservative leaders who have aided and abetted Romney's resiliency (see *We Won't Get Fooled Again: Where the Christian Right Went Wrong and How to Make America Right Again*).

One who was once fooled by Romney was the late, great Paul Weyrich—one of the founding fathers of the modern conservative movement. He supported Romney during his first presidential run in 2008, but when confronted with Romney's record that got him labeled the #8 RINO in the country by *Human Events* one year before Romney launched his campaign, Weyrich publicly repented in a room of his peers before he died. Now *that* kind of character is presidential.

Reagan's rising tide lifts all boats. Romney's race to the bottom takes others down with him. That's the difference between a Republicrat and a warrior, albeit an imperfect one.

We cannot demand perfection from imperfect vessels, but we must insist on consistency. We must provide encouragement and accountability to those who earnestly want to do what is right, and cease trusting those whose sell-out actions speak louder than their conservative words.

Republicrats would rather lose to Democrats than lose control of the GOP to grassroots conservatives or Libertarians like us. A friend of mine who is working on recruiting conservatives across the country to primary Republicrat incumbents once told me this: "The difference between Democrats and Republicans is Democrats look for ways to fire up and engage their base to get what they want. But Republicans look for ways to do an end run around their base to get what they want."

That last paragraph will be very provocative, and perhaps too much unvarnished truth to swallow in one instant for some of you. But you don't have to just take my word for it. You can take it directly from a top Republican strategist named Boyd Marcus.

The story of Boyd Marcus proves the GOP's betrayal of its base now runs so deep and has become so obvious that the ruling class of the Republican Party isn't even trying to lie to us anymore. They are just parading their whorish shamelessness out in the open and putting it right in our faces.

In 2013 Boyd Marcus decided to take a job working for Democrat Terry McAuliffe,[47] who was running for governor of Virginia. That's the same Terry McAuliffe who is the former chairman of the Democrat National Committee. That's the same Terry McAuliffe who has been a prolific fundraiser for the Democrat Party and its liberal causes for decades, including being the top fundraiser for the Clintons in the 1990s. That's the same McAuliffe that Louisiana Governor Bobby Jindal called on Democrats to drop as their gubernatorial candidate[48] after one of his companies was revealed to be under investigation from the SEC for its soliciting of foreign investors.

The bottom line is you don't get any more Democrat than Terry McAuliffe, and that's who top Republican strategist Boyd Marcus decided to go work for.

---

47 Erick Erickson, "Another GOP Strategist Working Against the GOP," *Red State*, August 20, 2013, http://www.redstate.com/2013/08/20/another-gop-strategist-working-against-the-gop/

48 James Hohmann, "Bobby Jindal Turns Up the Heat on Terry McAuliffe," *Politico*, August 5, 2013, http://www.politico.com/story/2013/08/virginia-terry-mcauliffe-bobby-jindal-95169.html

When I say Marcus was a top Republican strategist, consider that he counted among his clients Congressman Eric "don't defund Obamacare but do pass amnesty" Cantor, the House Majority Leader at the time this book was written. Marcus also worked for Bill Bolling, the former Lt. Governor of Virginia. Bolling was the Republican establishment's choice to be the GOP nominee for governor in 2013, but the grassroots went with State Attorney General Ken Cuccinelli instead. A bitter Bolling did little to hide his disdain for the conservative Cuccinelli,[49] and his top consultant went to work to get the Democrat elected. By the way, notice there were no sanctimonious cries from the Republican Party ruling class for Bolling and his supporters to get on board and unify to defeat the Democrat as conservatives are often lectured, but I digress.

Marcus isn't a RINO. Marcus isn't a moderate. He's a Republicrat. He doesn't represent the "the stupid party" as we have preferred to describe them because that spoonful of sugar helps the medicine go down, rather than us admitting what we really know the truth to be. And that truth is people like Marcus are actively working to help the other team score points, and any competitor knows that whoever scores points for your opponent is really your opposition no matter which jersey they're wearing at the time.

Marcus helped McAuliffe defeat one of the most promising emerging pro-liberty politicians in America. But he wasn't alone.

The Republican Governor's Association did almost nothing to help Cuccinelli[50], choosing to help the liberal Chris Christie win his 2013 race in New Jersey that he was never going to lose instead. The Republican National Committee bragged about giving Cuccinelli three million dollars, but that was one-third the money it

---

49 "Bolling Won't Endorse Cuccinelli; Rips Him as 'too extreme, combative, and controversial'," Blue Virginia, March 30, 2013, http://www.bluevirginia.us/diary/9007/audio-bolling-wont-endorse-cuccinelli-says-opposition-came-from-more-extreme-elements-of-gop

50 Matt Lewis, "Cuccinelli adviser blames Bobby Jindal, RGA for defeat: 'They just blew it'," The Daily Caller, November 6, 2013, http://dailycaller.com/2013/11/06/cuccinelli-advisor-blames-bobby-jindal-rga-for-defeat-they-just-blew-it/

gave his predecessor Bob McDonnell to run in 2009[51]. I even had a friend of mine at the RNC tell me he knew for a fact several big donors withheld money to the RNC until after Cuccinelli lost, because they wanted to make sure none of their money went to help him.

The story of of the betrayal of Cuccinelli (and thus the grassroots) in the 2013 Virginia governor's race will prompt more reactions like what happened in Maine after the 2012 election, when several members of the Republican State Central Committee (as well as a member of the Republican National Committee) resigned and left the Republican Party.[52] They cited Speaker John Boehner's "cowardly leadership" as well as "abandoning key principles for Libertarians and conservatives" as reasons for their departure. "The Republican Party has lost its way" they wrote.

You may disagree with how they've chosen to act on their assessment of the Republican Party (I am still active in party politics), but you'd have to be a complete party shill not to admit their assessment of the party's leadership is largely correct. So let's not blame those who acted on their convictions even if we don't agree with their actions. Let's put the blame where it belongs, on the Republicrats running the Republican Party who only care about their own self interest. They're the ones that continuously inspire us to abandon hope, all ye who enter here.

Boyd Marcus himself admitted the truth when he said he was working for McAuliffe because "he seems like the candidate willing to work with both parties to get things done."

Translation: Marcus actually agreed with McAuliffe more than he did Cuccinelli on the issues. Plus, McAuliffe isn't nearly the threat that a Cuccinelli was to the scam of gangster government people (like Boyd Marcus) who have been profiting off of for

51 Steve Deace, "Learn from Virginia," *Townhall*, November 9, 2013, http://townhall.com/columnists/stevedeace/2013/11/09/learn-from-virginia-n1742205

52 Kevin Miller, "Seven Members of Maine Republican Central Committee Leave Party," *Portland Press-Herald*, August 20, 2013, http://www.pressherald.com/news/Six-top-Maine-Republicans-quit-party.html

years. Marcus, a Republican strategist, wants to beat the Republican nominee for governor for all the reasons you would want someone like Cuccinelli elected.

It's time to stop lying to ourselves.

For too long we have come up with every explanation for why the GOP establishment fails (dumb, gutless, stupid, etc.) rather than accepting the simplest and most obvious one—these people are feckless operatives for the very worldview we became Republicans to defeat.

Republicrats don't mind being in the minority, because then they don't have to actually act on all the conservative clichés they spewed to get (and stay) elected. Huddling with their incestuous batch of bratty consultants to ponder the lint in their navels while the country falls apart is what they do best. Ignore whatever focus-driven filth called advice their political hacks provide you. Be very wary when they put their arm around you and talk about how many good ideas you have, but you'll probably have to table a few until the public is with you.

When they start asking you to lunch, that means you're having an impact and they're hoping that developing a rapport with you will get you to back down on your principles for the sake of maintaining the relationship. I can't tell you how many of these lunches I've wasted my time with the last few years. Talk, talk, talk. These Republicrats will talk you to death if you let them. As the great prophet Toby Keith once said, it's time for "a little less talk and a lot more action."

The most clear and present danger to the future of this republic is not Democrats, but Republicrats, because until we defeat Republicrats we're not even going to get a chance to defeat Democrats. Republicrats are why the American people don't trust us. We talk about limited government, but once in office limited government to Republicrats means limiting their political foes' access to the welfare state, but not their cronies'. The first step to defeating these people is to get more and more of our people involved in primaries and supporting principled, conservative candidates.

Otherwise we're quickly getting to the point that if the right kind of Republican doesn't win the primary it almost doesn't matter who wins the general election.

3

Never Attack What You're Not Willing to Kill

f you're going to win in politics you have to know what politics actually is.

Most of us believe politics is simply how we advance public policy in America, or cynically define it the way Obi-Wan Kenobi once defined the Mos Eisley spaceport in the original *Star Wars*: "You will never find a more wretched hive of scum and villainy." Those may be examples of what politics *does* or politics *becomes*, but that's not what politics *is*.

Politics is primarily two things.

First, politics is faith and ethics in action. A study done by a University of Virginia psychologist said Americans today are the most politically polarized we've ever been in our history, and the primary reason for the polarization is a difference in morality. What determines our morality? Our faith and ethics.

We are all, whether we prefer to recognize it or not, created in the image of the living God. From that common origin come similarities in our design despite differing ancestries. For instance, all human beings—unless they've had a complete psychological break and become psychopaths—work through the same philosophical paradigm when making any moral decision.

It begins with a faith/authority statement. In other words, the first thing we process is who or what we believe we are ultimately accountable to at the time, and/or the most in need of pleasing. That determination will dictate a belief system whereas we create an ideology to satisfy that faith/authority statement. That belief system will determine our convictions (i.e. behaviors, emotions, responses, thoughts, etc.), which are the actions we take in order to please and/or honor who or what we originally decided we either needed to please and/or be held accountable to.

This is why people say things like "actions speak louder than words" because how you act is what demonstrates to people whom or what you ultimately serve. A famous line in the Bible puts it this way: "Show me your faith apart from your works and I will show you my faith *by* my works."

When asked by his followers how will we know who is and isn't really one of us, Jesus didn't say "by their ability to clearly and consistently articulate a systematic theology you will know them." Rather, Jesus said "by their fruit you will know them." The fruit in question here is the kind that blossoms after a seed has been planted, grown deep roots, and then becomes a fully developed tree or crop. Someone may claim rather convincingly they intend to have an apple orchard, but if they plant a bunch of oranges instead they end up with a grove.

Likewise, someone can claim to be a conservative, Christian, Constitutionalist, loving father and husband, etc. all they want. But for others to believe that is true means there needs to be fruit or works that are indicative of what is expected from someone claiming to be any or all of those things.

This is why politicians who try to have it both ways by saying things like "I'm personally pro-life but I can't impose my private religious beliefs on others" are lying, phony hypocrites at best and schizophrenics at worst. If someone really believed that all human life comes from the Creator and is therefore sacred, they would do everything within their grasp to defend it short of succumbing to tactics that make them exactly like what they claim to be against.

Men, imagine if you came home and told your wife you were "personally pro-faithfulness but you can't impose your private religious beliefs on other women who might be attracted to you." The next call you'd need to make would either be your lawyer or a Kevlar distributor.

So let's apply this philosophical paradigm to politics. When a politician or candidate is faced with a moral dilemma the first thing he/she will do is determine who/what am I ultimately accountable to. This is a faith (or sometimes lack thereof) statement.

Am I ultimately accountable to my sworn oath of office? When I said "so help me God" who is that God and what does he/she/it demand of me?

Is it my own conscience I'm accountable to? What informs my conscience, and how do I know it should?

Is it my constituents? Do I do what my constituents want me to do even if I think its wrong? If there's a conflict between my conscience and the desires of my constituents, how do I decide which comes first, and how do I know that's right? Do I please the voters at all costs?

Is it the Constitution? How do I know my interpretation of the Constitution is correct? Then, how do I know the standard I chose to determine my interpretation of the Constitution is the right one?

Is it popular opinion like polls or the media pundits?

However he/she answers these questions will determine the belief system they will program into their sub-conscience to begin carrying out whatever eventual convictions (or lack thereof) they believe will get the approval of whom or what they're most trying to please.

So from now on when you hear a politician/candidate say they can separate their private religious beliefs from their public governance, realize that's because their private religious beliefs are really either non-existent or a steaming pile of horse puckey, otherwise they'd be driving their public convictions. What they act upon is what they really believe, because what they really believe is what drives them to do whatever it is they do (or don't).

And that's the same for you, me, your spouse, your children, your parents, your friends, and your boss; and for every other created being in all walks of life everywhere and at all times unless they've suffered some sort of psychotic break.

Along the same lines, many of our politicians/candidates fall into the trap of "will I do something" as opposed to asking themselves "can I do something?" Human nature is not basically good. Therefore, when we rely on our will, we are playing Russian Roulette with our ethics. For example, suppose I am locked in a room with an attractive, naked, and willing woman. At first I may not succumb to the temptation, but the more and more I ask myself "will I cheat on my wife" in this sort of situation the more likely I eventually will.

Many of the people we elect are facing a similar and daily den of iniquity once they're in public office. And the more they rely on their own will, the more their resolve will wear down and they will compromise, rationalize, or just surrender.

However, if I put myself in that same situation with that same attractive, naked, and willing woman, but then ask myself "can I cheat on my wife" instead, now the entire conversation within my conscience has changed, because can is a word that denotes permission. Do I have permission to disappoint my children in such a way? Do I have permission to betray my wife and everyone that counts on me? Do I have permission to break God's commandment against adultery?

Think I'm naïve? Think again. How many times have you gotten angry at a fellow driver's incompetence or rudeness on the road, and thought about running him down and letting him have it? So why don't you do it? Because your conscience pricks you by asking you "can you do that?"

That compels you to then count the cost of this action. You could put others in the car with you that you care about in danger. You could make yourself late for where you have to be next. You could do something that will cause you to be arrested and go to jail. In other words, by asking yourself "can I run this guy down" you have begun considering the consequences of your actions. If you ask yourself "will I run this guy down" you begin considering all the ways you would like to, thus feeding the desires of your fallen base nature and increasing the likelihood you will do some dangerous and/or dumb.

Imagine if our politicians asked themselves "can I violate my oath of office" as opposed to "will I violate my oath of office," or "can I go back on my word" as opposed to "will I go back on my word?" Many times I have been asked to do things that compromise my integrity, and sometimes these are things I would like to do if it were up to me alone.

But it's not. I am eternally accountable to my Creator, who redeemed me at the high cost of His own Son. I am accountable to my wife, whom I made a lifelong commitment to. I am accountable to my children, who need me to set a good example for them at the risk of making a mistake that could cost the generations that follow. I am accountable to my employees and business partners, who are banking on my integrity as part of my on-air persona. I am accountable to my audience, who needs to trust that what they're hearing coming over the radio each broadcast day is sincere.

Thus, when these temptations come my way I respond "I can't do it" and not "I won't do it." It's nothing personal, you're just asking me to do something I can't do. I have a defined boundary here, and I can no more violate that boundary than I can violate the boundary of my neighbor's yard and start treating it as my own.

This is why I will often ask those running for office "what can't you do?" The 10 Commandments God gave to Moses mainly consist of statements telling us what not to do, thus if we're going to honor the oath we swear to that same God we ought to have a pretty good idea of what we can't do as well.

Now that we've established the why and how politics is first and foremost faith and ethics in action, let's move on to the second thing politics is—how we conduct civil war in this country.

When we (conservatives, Christians, constitutionalists, Libertarians—all those that make up the right-of-center coalition in this country) view politics as a simple debate over public policy, and not how we conduct civil war in this country, we will lose every time. The other side understands this, which is why they ruthlessly pursue their agenda and worldview with far less concern for public opinion than we do.

We, on the other hand, want to debate, vent, wring our hands, or worse—nice the system to death. I especially see this among many of the Christian political circles I run in as a fellow Jesus freak. We're sending chaplains off to war when we should be sending soldiers trained to win the peace. The Bible says "blessed are the peacemakers" but it doesn't say "blessed are the peace lovers." Jesus himself said he came "not to bring peace but a sword."

After all, is there a message more confrontational and offensive in all of human history than the Gospel:

"You're evil. You crave and desire sin, and wouldn't do what's right unless there was something in it for you. You deserve hell for breaking God's commandments, and it is hell you will receive unless you accept through faith the grace that is offered through the exclusive truth of the redemptive work of Jesus Christ."

If someone can think of a "nice" way to tell every human being that has ever lived what I just wrote, by all means clue me in because as someone that communicates for a living I haven't discovered it yet. That might be why they hung Jesus on a cross and killed all of His apostles except one, whom they also tried to kill by boiling him in oil but he survived.

America's largest Christian church and its nicest and most well-known pastor, Joel Osteen, are in Houston, Texas. Joel smiles a lot. Okay, he smiles an awful lot, like perpetually. It's kind of creepy, really. But, hey, he's helping Americans find "their best life now" so who am I to judge?

But here's a question: if he and his church that is so large they have to meet in the basketball arena the NBA's Houston Rockets used to play in were really preaching the full truth of the Bible, would their city have elected their first lesbian mayor in 2009?

In fact, Osteen provided the prayer of blessing for the new lesbian mayor at her swearing-in ceremony.[53] There is no Biblical precedent in either the Old or New Testaments for a man of God enabling and validating that which God says is wrong so publicly. Jesus ate with sinners, but he died for their sins so they could be redeemed from their sinfulness, not blessed in it.

If it's true the "Black Robed Regiment" of pastors preaching freedom and liberty from America's pulpits were instrumental in our victory in the War for Independence, then it must also be true that too many of our pastors and pulpits are to blame for America's current nosedive towards Gomorrah and socialism by preaching watered down self-esteem psychobabble. We can't have it both ways.

As Alexis De Tocqueville said:

"I sought for the key to the greatness of America in her harbors; in her fertile fields and boundless forests; in her rich mines and vast world commerce; in her public school system and institutions of learning. I sought for it in her democratic Congress and in her matchless Constitution. Not until I went into the churches of America and heard her pulpits aflame with righteousness did I understand the secret of her genius and power. America is great because America is good, and if America ever ceases to be good, America ceases to be great."

That doesn't mean we look for needless ways to be offensive, any more than it means a soldier in combat indiscriminately kills civilians without just cause. Soldiers that do so are rightfully court-martialed, and those of us that are recklessly destructive in politics should be similarly reprimanded.

But war, if it's a just war, has been a constructive tool to administer justice and protect life, liberty, and property from the time Moses and Joshua commandeered the Israelites into the Promised Land. It was just war that defeated Adolph Hitler, and it was just

---

53 Cathy Lynn Grossman, "Joel Osteen Blesses Houston's New (Gay) Mayor," *USA Today,* January 5, 2010, http://content.usatoday.com/communities/Religion/post/2010/01/joel-osteen-annise-parker-gay-rights-evangelical/1#.Ul4xilAjJXY

war that drove the Red Coats from our shores. Just war should always be a last resort, but it should always be an available one when all other means are exhausted.

However, even a just war comes with an all too real and tragic human toll. That's what is so unique about America's political system, despite all its flaws. Most of the time in human history when a society can no longer come to a consensus on the definition of its most basic institutions and rights, it leads to coup d'état or civil war. Even our nation, which has the longest-standing Constitution in human history, has been unable to avoid such bloodshed in our past.

Thankfully, we usually end up resolving these disputes at the ballot box, with minimal casualties. The one exception to that has been child killing via abortion, where the casualties now exceed 50 million and counting.

Politics is a substitute for civil war, and it's also a variation of it. For further evidence just look at the terminology we often use in talking about the nuts and bolts of politics, like a campaign "war chest" or "propaganda." Those are terms of warfare.

If the generations preceding the Civil War had been more principled in utilizing the political process to end the abomination of slavery, perhaps it would've never come to war and the proper interpretation of the 10th Amendment protecting these United States from the endless encroachment of the federal government would've been preserved. The current understanding of federal supremacy over the states has its historical origins in the aftermath of the Civil War, as the federal government felt compelled to intervene on behalf of stopping the abomination of slavery. But now the feds call any assertion of the sovereignty of the states an excuse to impose further.

Likewise, if those of us who believe in the "American View" (to borrow a phrase from my friends at the Institute on the Constitution) enshrined in The Declaration of Independence—there is a God, our rights come from Him, and government's only duty and obligation is to protect those God-given rights—do not take advantage of the political process to restore the republic, then we may one day get another tragic reminder that those who do not learn from history are doomed to repeat it.

Throughout human history there has never been a mass government intrusion into individual wealth, property, and civil rights without bloodshed. We are wired by our Creator for survival, and that survival instinct kicks in when our very survival is threatened. Historically speaking, people do not just sit there and take it while there freedoms are threatened if they have other options. Anyone else notice the spike in the sales of firearms the past few years?

And neither should we. But we are blessed to have methods and tactics at our disposal that allows us to fight wars to stop the shedding of blood, not perpetuate it. I believe we have a moral obligation to take advantage of that, but no war is won by nicing the enemy to death.

To paraphrase George C. Scott's famous film portrayal of General Patton: "You don't win a war by dying for your cause, you win a war by making the other son of a gun die for his."

To make the other son of a gun die for his cause in politics you have to beat him in the arena of ideas, and then casualties are inflicted at the ballot box. Notice I didn't say maiming or wounding. I said casualties. A maimed or wounded enemy is among the most dangerous, for he has nothing to lose.

A dead enemy is a former enemy. Gone and soon forgotten. In combat you win by inflicting devastation and casualties upon your enemy on such a massive scale that you either annihilate them or they quit. That's why warfare requires a just cause, because if you can't morally justify that level of mass devastation then do not go to war. Trying to fight it more amicably just gets more of your own people (and innocent bystanders) killed.

It is the same in politics.

Right now in America we have one side playing to win, and another side playing not to lose. One side plays chess, the other side plays checkers. One side is fighting a war, the other side is posturing. Nationally, our side has been in a prevent defense pretty much since Reagan left office, and any good football fan knows the prevent defense just prevents you from winning.

One notable exception would be the Republican Revolution of 1994, which didn't last past 1996. George W. Bush won the presidency in 2000 (but lost the popular vote to Al Gore, which is hard to do) playing prevent defense with Karl Rove's empty "compassionate conservative" talking points. As we now know, Bush grew government more than any president in history up until that point, which eventually gave rise to true leftists like Nancy Pelosi as Speaker and Barack Obama as President.

We won the battle (beating the Democrats), but lost the war (restoring the republic). Then came 2010 and we took it upon ourselves to take on the system, cleaning house of several high-profile Republicrats in primaries and firing over 700 Democrats nationwide during those mid-term elections.

But then once in office some of those same grassroots conservatives we just got elected didn't take long to disappoint us. A 2012 Club for Growth study[54] found that Tea Party freshmen voted as a group about the same as the more moderate GOP leadership we sent them there to challenge.

Furthermore, CNS reported in June of 2012 the Republican-led House of Representatives increased federal spending "more in less than one term of Congress than in the first 97 Congresses combined."[55]

Gutless Republican Speaker John Boehner always attempts to excuse this tomfoolery by saying they're just one half of one-third of the government. Except that's nonsense. The Constitution says that all appropriations (i.e. spending) begins in the House, which means the federal government is not allowed to allocate a penny of our money without first getting approval for it from the chamber Boehner presides over.

---

54 Jim Galloway, "Club for Growth: 'Tea Party' Class of 2010 No Different Than Predecessors," *Atlanta Journal-Constitution,* May 15, 2012, http://blogs.ajc.com/political-insider-jim-galloway/2012/05/15/club-for-growth-%E2%80%98tea-party%E2%80%99-class-of-2010-no-different-than-predecessors/

55 Terrence Jeffrey, "Debt Up 1.5T Under GOP House, More in 15 Months than First 97 Congresses Combined," CNS News, June 1, 2012, http://cnsnews.com/news/article/debt-159t-under-gop-house-more-15-months-first-97-congresses-combined

Boehner and his colleagues could've thrown a monkey wrench into all of Obama's schemes if they wanted to, including the de-funding of Obamacare and Planned Parenthood. There's a reason why the Speaker of the House is second in line to the presidency, because it's one of the most powerful positions in the U.S. Government.

Except Boehner and his enablers in the Republican caucus aren't soldiers, they're bureaucrats. The difference is a soldier takes territory while a bureaucrat protects his own. We need more soldiers who inflict casualties upon the enemy because they don't stop shooting until the body stops twitching (metaphorically speaking of course).

Soldiers don't negotiate with the enemy, they provoke him to surrender. When was the last time Boehner and his colleagues got the Democrats to surrender on anything? Heck, when was the last time the Republican Party's national leadership got the Democrats to surrender on anything for that matter?

Our civilization doesn't have the time to wait for Boehner and his colleagues to take the advice God once gave to Job when He said "gird your loins like a man." If a man hasn't discovered his testicular fortitude by the time he's 62 years-old, it's not likely to happen. We need to start replacing the Boehners of this world with soldiers, and soldiers know you never attack what you're not willing to kill.

John McCain was once a soldier of tremendous valor, but over the course of his career in politics he became a liberal-media pandering maverick who went out of his way to betray conservatives (and thus the country) over and over again. One issue McCain did consistently fight on was pork barrel spending. Yet when the TARP (which pollster Scott Rasmussen says is the most unpopular legislation in recent American history) emerged down the stretch of his 2008 presidential run, he suspended his campaign to aid and abet the passage of the very kind of corrupt spending he fought against his entire career.

Mitt Romney once had the brass tacks to make billion-dollar deals as a global financier without blinking, putting his and countless others' very livelihoods at stake each and every time. But he's run for office four times and each time he ran as someone totally different. In 1994 he ran for U.S. Senate in Massachusetts as anti-Reagan and to the left of Ted Kennedy on social issues. In 2002 he ran for governor of Massachusetts as a make-the-trains-run-on-time, blue-state Republican. His official portrait as governor depicts him signing into law Romneycare, which was the fore-runner and blueprint for the Obamacare he now claims to oppose. In 2008 Romney ran for president as a Reagan conservative, trying to get to the right of Mike Huckabee despite his previous campaigns and record. In 2012 he ran for president as an establishment heir apparent.

Pick a persona, Mitt, any persona. And some politicians wonder why they lack credibility with the American people.

What's funny about Mitt McCain is that after spending their political careers pandering to liberals and selling out their base, once they secured the Republican presidential nomination they ended up drowning in all the same haterade the liberal media labels any true conservative with.

McCain was for *Roe v. Wade* most of his senate career—including his 2000 presidential run—and has always been for government funding of embryonic stem cell research that pro-lifers oppose. A technology that is complete liberal mythology and has yet to save any lives, but has destroyed many. Nonetheless, all the pro-child killing groups were just as vociferous in characterizing him as "anti-reproductive freedom" as they would've been a life-long pro-lifer like a Huckabee.

Romney's original tax plan was called "timid" by the conservative-leaning *Wall Street Journal* during the 2012 primary, and even included the very patronizing targeted tax cuts to appease the class warfare crowd the Left often panders to. Yet all those same class warfare groups demagogued Romney for his wealth (see that as success) as they would've any rich white Republican like Steve Forbes, who actually advocated a ballsy overhaul of the liberals' entire tax-and-spend scheme when he ran for president. Remember when Romney got unfairly panned for his 47% comment? Turns out that's exactly what he ended up with in the 2012 popular vote.

The Mitt McCains of the world waste their entire political careers declaring "peace in our time" with the enemy, desperately trying to show them they're not like those dastardly conservatives they despise. Then once they reach the summit, the liberal enemy they spent all those years pandering to pummels them with the exact same blitzkrieg of political propaganda they would pound any principled conservative with.

In contrast to Mitt McCain are Ronald Reagan and Scott Walker.

Former President Reagan attacked the Soviet Union with the intent to kill it. He didn't want to peacefully coexist with totalitarianism, nor regulate it incrementally out of existence. He wasn't satisfied with fewer nations under the Iron Curtain. He wanted to defeat it. Even over the objection of his own advisors, Reagan attacked the Soviet Union at its root, famously labeling the Soviet Union as "the evil empire" in a speech to the National Religious Broadcasters in his first term. With the aid of the late former British Prime Minister Margaret Thatcher and the late Pope John Paul II, Reagan launched a full-scale cold war to dismantle Sovietism. By the time Reagan left office the Soviet Union's influence was declining, and "the evil empire" collapsed just two years later.

Faced with presiding over the Midwest's version of California, or total statewide insolvency, Wisconsin Governor Scott Walker did what the man who played "the Terminator" in the movies didn't have the guts to do when he was governor of a state going broke. Arnold Schwarzenegger issued IOUs to the taxpayers. Walker took on the government sector employee unions who for too long had called the shots in state government at the expense of the taxpayers. He faced them down, even at the risk of his own recall, and routed them. His goal wasn't to be a little less bankrupt, or a little less ruled by the Leftist mobocracy, his goal was to defeat them.

Which type of leader would you rather have? Which type of leader do you think America needs more of? Since today's American Leftists have much in common with the totalitarian regimes in the former Soviet Union and China (statism, child killing on demand, anti-Christian, anti-liberty, coddling dictators and Islamic radicalism, etc.), I see no reason to restrain ourselves from treating them accordingly. If these folks get their way, our entire civilization will be undone. We can't be a little bit pagan. We can't be a little bit statist. We're either the America we were founded to be or we are not.

One of the dumbest things in football is a receiver getting what's called "alligator arms," which means the receiver didn't fully extend his arms to catch the ball because he anticipated he was going to get hit hard by the defensive player if he did. Except more often than not the defensive player is behind the receiver, so he can't tell if he actually caught the ball or not. That's why defensive players are coached to hit the receiver anyway in anticipation of breaking up the pass. Thus, it's never made any sense to me why a receiver would get alligator arms, since he's going to get hit just as hard regardless. If you're going to get hit anyway, why not fully extend your arms to make the catch to make the pain worth it?

We need political soldiers who count the cost of *not* doing something at least as much as they count the cost *of* doing something. A receiver who counts the cost of getting hit gets alligator arms, but a receiver who counts the cost of not making the catch fully extends to make the play. Likewise, a politician who counts the cost of being criticized by those that will never support him anyway will buckle, but a politician who counts the cost of not defending Constitutional principles will stand firm.

That's why never attack what you're not willing to kill is one of the first commandments of political warfare. If you only shoot to injure your enemy, he doesn't try to kill you less once he heals and gets back on the battlefield because you didn't kill him the first time.

No, he comes back with a vengeance. You will get no credit from him for showing restraint, so you at might as well go for the metaphorical kill-shot (see that as the win).

If we do not learn and put into practice this commandment, then there's no need proceeding further. Trying to fight a war without trying to win just makes things even worse. You're actually better off doing nothing. If you're supporting a candidate or a cause that isn't willing to play to win, you're wasting your time as well as the future for your children and grandchildren.

And time is the one thing they're not making more of.

4

Never Accept the Premise of Your Opponent's Argument.

Premise is a word many Americans are not familiar with, and neither do they use it in their everyday speech. However, the premise is one of the most powerful weapons in political warfare. Master the art of the premise, and you will master your opponent.

A premise is the assumption of an argument that is meant to justify the conclusion the one making the argument is hoping you'll come to. If one fails to establish the premise to his argument, one almost always fails to convince others of his conclusion. On the other hand, if one establishes a premise one will more than likely get others to agree with his conclusion.

For example, if the premise of the argument is over "reproductive choice" and not "the sanctity of human life," then the conclusion will come down on the side of the premise accepted. If there's one thing the Republicrats are good at, it's accepting the Left's premise on virtually everything. As a result, for too long we have argued with the Left over the conclusion (e.g. big government vs.

small government) when we should be arguing the premise (e.g. what's legal for the government to do vs. what's illegal for the government to do).

Thankfully there were plenty of grassroots patriots who have read the Constitution that could invade many of the town halls held by the ruling class in the summer of 2009 and attack their flawed premise. These town halls became a treasure trove of sound bites for talk show hosts like me, with the ruling class caught on tape saying all kinds of stupid and anti-constitutional things. This set the stage for the midterm uprising of 2010, when several Republicrats were defeated in primaries and more than 700 Democrats nationwide were fired by the American people at the polls.

This was all done in spite of the leadership of the Republican Party, not because of it. We had to drag the GOP leadership kicking and screaming across the finish line.

While we were basing our arguments against Obamacare on the law of the land, the Republican Party establishment was relying on shallow talking points like "we can't afford it." It's tough to argue "we can't afford it" when the other side is arguing on behalf of every contrived class of victims in the culture. If you were a politician, would you rather be Ebenezer Scrooge or Robin Hood?

On the other hand, if you argue the legality of legislation rather than its supposed good intentions, the entire argument is re-framed in your favor. Because if the basis for government action in our system is simply good intentions, then what *can't* the government do? Moreover, what or who determines which and whose intentions are "good?" Every despot and dictator believes his intentions are good, and alternative definitions for good intentions have led to some of the wickedest government in history.

Our Founding Fathers knew this, so they accomplished a first in the history of mankind—a Constitution that binds the jurisdiction and conscience of the state, rather than the individual. Prior to our Constitution, governments issued legal documents to clearly define the rights of citizens, and operated under the premise all rights and privileges came from government. Our Constitution begins with the premise that our rights come from

God, and that government's only role is to secure and protect those God-given rights.

For example, since God grants all people the right to call on Him ("whoever calls on the name of the Lord shall be saved") when their hearts are convicted to do so, our government has an obligation to protect your religious freedom. Another example might be since God grants us the right to self-defense, our government has an obligation to protect and enforce the Second Amendment.

The Constitution is a plainly-worded, objective moral standard of self-governance. It is no more a living, breathing document than is the Bible, and it's no coincidence the same people who believe the Bible is open to their subjective whims believe the same of the Constitution. Once someone defies God's authority, defying man's authority is no big deal.

We are not predicated on the rule of victims, but the rule of law. Our Founders loathed the term "democracy" for a reason, because it has a penchant to devolve into mob rule. This is why they established a republic, where our elected officials are not our rulers or leaders but rather our representatives/employees. Since their opportunity to govern comes only from the consent of the governed, we are in essence utilizing them as our proxies. And the power we have afforded them we can take back and give to someone else if they're not doing the job we want them to do.

Our Founders read in the Bible where it says, "Do not pervert justice; do not show partiality to the poor or favoritism to the great, but judge your neighbor fairly." We're not to be intimidated by someone of great wealth and influence, nor are we to be emotionally manipulated by the downtrodden. What we are to do is perpetuate a government where there is no caste system, but rather everyone is held accountable to the same standard no matter their station in life, and everyone has an equal opportunity to pursue happiness.

Another group of people once rose to power promising their own government-imposed definition of fairness. They were called Bolsheviks. In America we promise the freedom to exploit your God-given talent to its fullest potential, and you face the consequences for failure and reap the rewards of success.

Which system would you rather defend?

Let's take a look at several key economic questions facing the country right now for some examples of not accepting the Left's premise.

I was asked by a website to join an esteemed list of contributors, most of whom are smarter and more well-known than me, in an ongoing conversation about some of the hot-button economic issues facing the country.

With folks representing the Cato Institute, Club for Growth, and Stanford University, as well as names like Dinesh D'Souza, Grover Norquist, Star Parker, and James Taranto having already answered the site's questions, I was wondering what it is I could possibly contribute to the conversation that hadn't already been said?

That's when it dawned on me that often debates about the future of the country immediately jump to the conclusion of our worldview, when we should be arguing the premise.

For example, we argue for limited government when the real argument is *why* someone is for small government or big government. Drawing this distinction is more important than ever before, because there is a debate within conservative circles about whether limited government and freedom can occur in a vacuum apart from addressing the moral issues or the condition of the culture.

And the answer to that question is absolutely not.

You cannot have limited/self-government without first having a moral people capable of governing themselves, and you cannot have a moral people without the sort of spiritual awakening in a culture that preceded this republic in the first place. It's no coincidence the more we collectively turn our backs on our spiritual heritage, the more immoral the culture becomes, and thus the bigger government gets.

For if men will not be ruled by God they must be ruled by other men, otherwise there's no higher authority we can call upon to settle our disputes and disagreements with one another. The more we need the rule of man, the bigger the government gets. The more we submit to the rule of God, the smaller the government gets.

With this in mind, I decided to answer their questions from a worldview standpoint rather than attempt to discuss tactical economics with those who know a lot more about it than I do. If we cannot challenge the premise of the Left's belief system we cannot deconstruct it, and if we can't deconstruct it we certainly will not be able to defeat it. Currently, we are not challenging the Left's premise, we are venting about the conclusion/application of their premise.

Read the questions and then my answers to get an idea of what it means to never accept the premise of your opponent.

What Causes an Economy to Prosper?

The most prosperous economies are those that truly understand the role of government. As it is stated in our founding document, The Declaration of Independence: there is a God, our rights come from Him, and the only purpose of government is to secure and defend those God-given rights. To put it another way, government is to encourage (not do) good and punish evil. Of course, government in and of itself is not a moral agent, and usually inflicts the most horrors on humanity when it attempts to be, so it needs another institution to define for it what is good and what is evil. That is the role of the church and the family. These clearly defined spheres of jurisdiction between cultural institutions are what produce the proper balance of liberty and morality, thus allowing for the most prosperity.

What Role Should Government Play in an Economy?

The biggest misconception is that we're having a debate about the role of government in America today, when we're really having a debate about what authority or moral ethic are we going to govern ourselves by. The answer to that question then determines the role of government. For example, cultures that abandon the Judeo-Christian moral ethic, as ours is currently doing, end up growing government because something must fill the God-shaped void (justice, law, education, validation, charity, etc.) in the society. And that something ends up being the state. As G.K. Chesterton once said, "When government removes God, government becomes god."

What Kind of Tax System is most effective?

The tax and monetary system that was in place in this country prior to 1913 (prior to the confiscatory federal income tax and the printing of a fiat currency) helped encourage the greatest growth of human freedom and prosperity the world had ever known. Since abandoning that foundation we have increasingly become a debtor nation/people. I may have gone to public school and not the Ludwig von Mises Institute of Advanced Austrian Libertarian Economics, but even I'm smart enough to know to go back to what worked before.

How do High Taxes on the Wealthy Impact an Economy?

Every job I've ever had came from a rich person, so I'm not sure how punitively punishing the very people who provide jobs will create more of them.

What is the Cause and Solution to Poverty?

The greatest way to combat poverty is to first recognize what causes it in the first place—sinful human nature. Sometimes that sinful human nature manifests itself as a robber baron who exploits the community's natural and human resources, thus making it harder if not impossible for his fellow man to maximize his God-given talent so he can provide for himself and his family. Sometimes that sinful human nature manifests itself in the wrongful choices individuals make that put their livelihood and property at risk.

Either way, this is the reason why God gave the church the primary role of distributing charity in human society, because ultimately the church has the moral message to confront the evils that cause poverty in the first place. When an amoral agent like the state intervenes instead, the best it can do is apply a band-aid to a flesh wound. It can treat the symptom, but it lacks the prescription to become the cure. Then, after a while, it becomes an enabler of the very thing it's trying to fix. Just like it is today.

What Role do Workers' Unions play in an Economy?

Human history has shown that whenever power is concentrated in the hand of a few, or just one, corruption is bound to take place regardless of the belief system of those (or the one) in whose hands the power lies. That's why historically unions played a vital role as a check and balance on unfettered corporate power. Obviously unions have also struggled with the same fallen nature manifested as corruption that corporatists have.

Nowadays, unfortunately, unions (particularly government sector unions) do not primarily serve the needs of their workers but are more or less a funding stream and campaign platform for the Democrat Party. So while the union bosses have a seat at the table, the workers are worse off.

How Does a Minimum Wage Requirement Impact an Economy?

How can a government know what the minimum wage should be? Can anyone even support a family on the minimum wage? Here is the reality: real wages in this country have declined in relation to the rate of inflation/debt since these sorts of government schemes to contrive equality began.

Our wages nowadays do not have the buying power in a consumer-driven economy they once had, which is one of the reasons we carry so much debt. Just about every major purchase a family makes these days is made on credit. These schemes are actually harming the very people they purport to help, because they're operating outside the natural laws of economics.

Let me give an example. Suppose a movie theater owner has calculated the job of popcorn attendant is worth $5/hour based on his business model and the current job market. In other words, based on finite, objective standards.

However, the government comes in and mandates he pay a minimum of $10/hour for that job instead under the subjective guise of "fairness." The movie theater owner doesn't just cut into his own profit margin to cover that increased cost out of the kindness of his own heart, but rather jacks up the price of popcorn to pass along his cost to the consumer. Now the market tethered by competition is no longer setting the price, but government artificially is.

That sounds well and good until you and I go to buy popcorn the next time we're at the theater, and we're still making the same amount of money we were making before the price got jacked up. Since we can't go back to our bosses and demand a raise to cover our popcorn habit, right away our buying power is diminished by this government intrusion into a consumer-driven economy. Not to mention so is the popcorn attendant's, because on his night off when he takes his date to the movies he'll notice he's making more money, but now this date is costing him more money, too. He's essentially being given the bill for his own minimum wage increase.

And he'll notice the same thing at the restaurant he takes her, too, and everywhere else where entry-level workers were given a completely contrived minimum wage increase. In other words, his minimum wage "increase" is at-best a revenue-neutral transaction once the arbitrary consumer price increase offsets the arbitrary minimum wage increase he got from Uncle Sam. Meaning at best he'll break even and most of the time it's a loss-leader.

This partially explains why the explosion in government since 2007 has led to a reduction in American wealth to 1992 levels. We're buying goods and services at 2012 prices with a standard of living that is 20 years old.

We have a saying on our radio show: why be in a hurry to be wrong?

I know our unwillingness to immediately comment on things

we actually haven't researched and analyzed frustrates some in this instant gratification world, but it also helps us sleep well at night and avoid looking as foolish as *The Huffington Post*.

Recent headlines say fast-food workers are demanding a "living wage" of $15/hour. Of course, how do we know that's actually a living wage? Why not demand $20/hour, or $50/hour, or even $100/hour? A full-time job that pays $15/hour comes out to $31,200 (not counting overtime) a year. Can you really live the American dream (own a home, own a car, send your kids to good schools and then eventually college, and one family vacation per year) on $31,200 per year? After all, the federal poverty line for a family of four is currently $23,550 per year, but I digress.

Of course, never wanting to miss an opportunity to play class warfare, outlets like *The Huffington Post* owned by Arianna Huffington (with a net worth of $35 million[56], so of course she identifies with the plight of the downtrodden), were overly eager to report as fact analysis of McDonalds' financials from an alleged "University of Kansas research assistant" named Arnobio Morelix.[57]

Morelix "reported" that if McDonald's immediately doubled all the wages of its employees, including the $9 million CEO, it would "only" have to raise the cost of a Big Mac by 68 cents, and it's "dollar menu" to $1.17/item. This comes out to a "measly" 17% price increase.

It all sounds well and good of course in magical thinking land, but there's one small problem—Morelix is full of shinola.

First of all, you can't on one hand imply McDonalds is a greedy corporation that refuses to pay its employees a living wage, and then fail to recognize that if McDonald's could get away with just arbitrarily raising their prices by 17% they already would've done it. Wouldn't the greedy corporation you're smearing actually be bilking employees *and* customers at the same time if they could?

---

56 http://www.celebritynetworth.com/richest-politicians/democrats/arianna -huffington-net-worth/

57 "Errors in McDonald's Wage Analysis," *The Huffington Post*, July 29, 2013, http:// www.huffingtonpost.com/2013/07/29/mcdonalds-salaries_n_3672006.html

Especially since customers pay into the business model, while employees are overhead that subtract from it? Hello, McFly . . . anybody home?

The reality is just as employees want to make more money so does the company. Employees would like to make $15/hour instead of $7.50, and McDonald's would like to charge $10 for a Big Mac instead of $3.99 as well. But McDonald's isn't the federal government, able to just print more money whenever it wants. McDonald's has to live within the natural laws of economics, which state you can't spend more than you have and if you don't make a profit you're out of business (and all the jobs are gone, too).

That simple application of common sense should have shown *The Huffington Post* that hitching its wagon to Morelix was a bridge to nowhere, but when thinking emotionally common sense is in short supply. We don't have time to think for ourselves, mind you, when we're too busy reporting the story we want to be true even if it's not.

It turns out Morelix isn't a "research assistant at the University of Kansas." He's actually just an undergraduate student there. When it printed its correction story, *The Huffington Post* said they ran with the story without fact-checking any of Morelix's so-called "data" themselves. For example, *The Huffington Post* said prior to publication they "asked Morelix if his analysis included franchises and he said it did."

My translation: "this college kid told us what we wanted to hear so we just took it at face value."

I wish my editors at places like *USA Today* would afford me the same courtesy when I submit a column. Instead, I routinely have to provide multiple sources for my assertions.

By the way, it turns out Morelix didn't factor in McDonalds' franchise business model, which accounts for more than 80% of McDonalds' restaurants worldwide

Oops.

Morelix also asserted McDonald's currently spends 17.1% of its revenues on labor when in reality it's almost double that.

Oops.

Since many McDonald's franchises are owned by small business owners (the average annual cash flow for a McDonald's franchise is only $275,000,[58] and the average franchise experiences 43% staff turnover each year),[59] doubling wages would actually require lay-offs. In addition, that's not even counting the impact of the Obamacare employee-mandate on these small businesses for employees working more than 30 hours a week.

Oops.

Furthermore, the typical household consuming McDonald's has an average annual income of $60,000/year or lower. Since at least one-third of the cost of increased wages would be passed on to customers, you're not promoting a "living wage" but really waging war on the middle class.

Oops.

I give credit to *The Huffington Post* for running a thorough correction, but the truth is this was an unnecessary hit to their credibility. All they had to do was look at what their owner does to maintain her wealth to realize they were being scammed.

Why do People disagree About the Truth?

Without an agreed upon fixed standard everyone becomes wise in his own eyes. Everybody believes their truth, which means somebody's truth isn't true. The fixed moral standard that once served this country well and made it the freest and most prosperous nation on the planet was the Judeo-Christian moral tradition. Since we have abandoned it the culture has become more immoral, government has grown uncontrollably, and many once treasured institutions and associations in this country have become corrupted.

---

58 http://www.burgerbusiness.com/?p=9385

59 http://www.hrcapitalist.com/2010/01/you-own-a-mcdonalds-franchise-how-much-would-you-pay-for-10-more-in-revenue.html

That pretty much settles the argument on what truth is actually true as far as I am concerned.

The question is whether or not there is enough humility remaining in this culture to admit we've deviated off the proper path and ask for directions back to the main (narrow) road.

Now you get an idea of what I'm talking about. As a conservative, are you more confident arguing the premise I just articulated in my answers to the above eight questions, or the phony "fairness" premise of the American Left?

That's what I thought.

All too often we accept the premise of the Left's argument on virtually every issue, which allows them to frame the political battlefield. Any good general will attempt to shape the battlefield in a manner that gives his soldiers the best chance at victory, and we should do the same in the culture war as well.

Could you imagine the possibilities if we made the Left defend the Constitutionality (see that as legality) of all their statist schemes, and if our Republican politicians asked questions that rejected their premise from the outset?

I get asked questions all the time from the Left's perspective, and I never accept their premise. For example, in 2011 I did an interview on Dutch National Television. One of the questions was whether those who practice homosexuality should be allowed to serve openly in the military.

"I believe all men and women that are physically qualified and able to conform to the Uniformed Code of Military Justice ought to be able to serve their country," I replied.

"But what about gays and lesbians," the Dutch host asked.

"I'm sorry, maybe you didn't hear me," I replied. "I believe all men and women that are physically qualified and able to conform to the Uniformed Code of Military Justice ought to be able to serve their country."

Now he looked confused. "So, is that a yes or a no?"

"There are only two types of people," I told him. "Men and women."

He had nowhere to go after that because I totally shut his premise down by rejecting it from the outset. From there I was on offense throughout the rest of the interview.

Recently I was asked by a newspaper reporter to comment on a story he was working on regarding the perception conservatives have a monopoly on the American flag and patriotism. The story centered around a liberal activist who was sewing into an American flag an anti-marriage/pro-immorality speech by Hillary Clinton as a protest against this perceived bias.

"Do you think the American flag is seen as a conservative symbol," he asked.

"The American flag is a symbol of the virtues and values the generation that devised it and died for it intended it to be, which they enshrined for future generations in the Declaration of Independence and U.S. Constitution," I replied. "Those virtues and values should defy labels except American. Unfortunately, as we cascade over the post-modern cliff, all such absolutes are now considered negotiable."

"Do you think it's appropriate to incorporate the flag into progressive/liberal messages like a pro-gay marriage art project," he followed up.

"I think our society is better off when we conform our beliefs to the virtues and value that define the American flag, rather than conforming what the flag stands for to suit our own personal whims, desires, and agendas," I answered.

"What's your response to the claim that conservatives have an unfair monopoly on the flag," he asked for his final question.

"It's clear from their own writings and actions what values and virtues our Founders intended the flag to stand for: there is a God, our rights come from Him, and the purpose of government is to protect those God-given rights," I responded. "That vision should transcend our current petty political labeling, and if your particular agenda doesn't reconcile with that uniquely American vision the problem is you, not the vision."

Nowhere in this dialogue did I accept the premise of the

questioning, which was that the country is so divided that we even have multiple interpretations of traditional Americana. Nothing could be further from the truth, for we do not get to interpret the meanings of such things when the authors themselves left such a clear record of what they meant.

That is Social Reconstructionism, and if I accept the premise of these questions I am accepting the validity of that pagan and un-American philosophy, which means we never arrive at the truth and just keep arguing our own perspectives.

If the Leftists want to make the case what they believe is in line with the founding vision of these United States, then by all means go back into the historical record and make that case. Except they won't and they can't. There's a simple reason why the Left doesn't pay as much homage to the founding of this country as we do, and it's because most of what they believe is contrary to it, which is why they've had to take over the schools and scrub that history from the textbooks. Even one of the Left's favorite Founding Fathers, Thomas Jefferson, was so conservative compared to what most liberals believe they'd peg him with their favorite word for conservatives—"extreme."

Proving yet again that whichever side's premise is argued in the argument almost always wins was McCain-Palin in 2008. During each of the debates that year, including the vice presidential showdown between Sarah Palin and Joe Biden, the Democrats argued the economic collapse happening at the time was the result of too much de-regulation when the exact opposite was true. Not once in any of those debates did McCain-Palin defend the free market, and they just accepted the premise of the Democrat's phony argument.

An economic crash from too much big government resulting in President Bush insanely "suspending free market principles to save the free market"[60] was the perfect time for the Republican presidential ticket to take the national witness stand on behalf of free

---

60 Americans for Prosperity, "Bush Says He Sacrificed Free Market Principles to Save the Economy," December 16, 2008, http://www.google.com/hostednews/afp/article/ALeqM5jyyKrPjYt7VhpS8G8DrRkr18B0hA?hl=en

enterprise. It gave McCain-Palin a chance to triangulate between the unpopular Democrat Congress and the unpopular, lame duck President Bush, and channel the angst of Joe the Plumber as our champions to take on the ruling class.

Instead, the premise of Obama-Biden that government wasn't tinkering with our economy enough was allowed to stand. In the minds of voters an attack unanswered or a premise unchallenged becomes true. So the American people took their cue from that and voted for more big government by voting for Obama-Biden.

And they've been suffering for it ever since.

Proving those who do not learn from history are doomed to repeat it, not once but twice during the 2012 presidential debates Mitt Romney failed to confront President Obama on his version of the events that led to four dead Americans at the Benghazi terror attacks. Romney allowed Obama's false premise to be asserted on the biggest stage of the campaign, thus allowing what should've been an issue that toppled the Obama presidency to become a strength prior to voters heading to the polls. It wasn't until after the election in Congressional hearings featuring several Benghazi whistle-blowers—all of whom who worked for Obama—that the president's account proved to be false. By then it was too late, and those four dead Americans and their families still haven't received justice as of the time this book was written.

One of the reasons we see so many Republicans accepting the premise of the Left's argument is because they don't possess a solid worldview. Thus, most Republicans end up being defined by what they're against and not what they're for. Without a premise they're just playing defense, and often end up opposing things like homo-sexuals marrying because it's icky, not because they have any prin-cipled basis for doing so. Once the Left exposes that, they cave on a moral issue like marriage because they can be exposed as hypo-crites for their own private sexual behavior.

Heck, most Republicans don't know what they're for beyond they're for beating Democrats.

The Left is always advancing their premise, and too many Republicans don't have one, which means unless we the people step in we end up allowing liberals to frame the argument. We can step in when it comes to voting, but at some point we need to actually elect politicians who can advance our premise in the arena of public policy. Otherwise we'll continue going "forward" over the cliff the Left has us headed towards.

The only debate will be how fast over that cliff we go.

5

Never Surrender the Moral High Ground

The charismatic preacher approaches the podium. The crowd eagerly anticipates his words of inspiration. Inwardly, they know their cause is just, but their external resolve needs one more proverbial boost of confidence from their leader before they carry on the fight for civil rights against discrimination and oppression. Anxiously awaiting their marching orders, they're stunned to hear their leader say:

> *Ladies and gentlemen, we know it is wicked and evil for a man created in the image of God to oppress his fellow image bearer just because the color of his skin is different. We know that our Declaration of Independence says 'all men are created equal,' which means we are all made in the image of Creator God, and are guaranteed freedom thusly. However, the courts have ruled in Dred Scott that we are property after all, and in* Plessey v. Ferguson *that separate but equal is the law of the land. Given that, until we control a majority of justices on the U.S. Supreme Court, we'll never be able*

to have civil rights. So in the meantime, we have to take the best deal that we can get. That's why today I'm urging you to back legislation that will stop the lynchings of the elderly. At the very least we can stop late-term discrimination, when even some vicious racists oppose the lynching of the infirm. We can't stop all discrimination, but half a loaf is better than none. Besides, the person who believes in equality 80% of the time isn't a 20% racist.

Boy, that'll preach! Way to fire up the troops there, coach! Does that sound like the bold vision and strategy that carried the civil rights movement to victory?

But before you start thinking my example sounds utterly asinine, which it does, keep in mind the hypothetical speech I just wrote has essentially been the message of the movement fighting against the most grave injustice in our contemporary society—the shedding of innocent blood.

There is nothing more evil for a culture to do than to turn its back on its most vulnerable and its next generation. Only a culture drowning in self-loathing would voluntarily extinguish its best and brightest before they're even born. Child killing via abortion has cost over 50 million Americans their lives in the past 40 years, which are more American casualties than every war this country has fought in combined.

Beyond the human toll is the societal one. Who knows which of those dead children might have one day discovered the cure for cancer, AIDs, or even the common cold? Or maybe have discovered a clean form of energy that sparked a second industrial revolution? On a smaller, more personal scale, who knows if one of those dead children would've saved you or a loved one's life one day? But now they won't be there to do that. I once saw a pro-education commercial pointing out that every high school drop-out had the potential to do something special for society, and now that they're gone from school that potential is essentially wasted given what happens to most drop-outs.

The same could certainly be said for every aborted baby as well. Not to mention this level of internal carnage rots away at the soul of a nation, to the point that life becomes less valued overall. In 2012 a jury in Portland, Oregon awarded a couple $3 million in a "wrongful birth" lawsuit,[61] because the hospital failed to prenatally identify their unborn child's disability. See, had they known their daughter was disabled they would've killed her ahead of time before she was born.

Our society is not only willing to turn its back on the most vulnerable among us, but also to slaughter them for profit. In the introduction I detailed just how lucrative the child killing business is. There is no negotiating with that level of man's inhumanity to man. Just as there was no negotiating with Jim Crowe, nor was there any negotiating with slavery. Yet negotiating with child killing is exactly what the pro-life movement has been doing for 40 years.

And by doing so it has surrendered the moral high ground of its moral crusade.

By focusing on regulating child killing, rather than focusing on defending the sanctity of human life, the pro-life movement/industry has raised untold millions of dollars for political activism, and has certainly contributed to the rapid decline of available abortion clinics in America today. [62]

But sadly we're not any closer to overturning *Roe v. Wade* then we were decades ago. That's because as pro-lifers we're actually not even arguing the sanctity of life most of the time, but the quality of life instead, which is actually the argument of the pro-aborts.

Pro-aborts use quality of life arguments to justify child killing. They ask questions like is the child wanted? Will the child be born with a disability? Will the child be born into poverty? Was the child conceived via rape or incest? Is the child's mother a drug addict that can't possibly take care of him? These are all utilitarian, quality of life questions.

---

61 Steve Deace, "The Worst Parents in America," *Townhall*, March 17, 2012, http://townhall.com/columnists/stevedeace/2012/03/17/the_worst_parents_in_america

62 Tom Strode, "Abortion Clinics Closing at Record Rate," *Christianity Today*, September 13, 2013, http://www.christianitytoday.com/gleanings/2013/september/abortion-clinics-closing-planned-parenthood-abby-johnson.html

Sadly, the pro-life movement/industry has largely adopted a similar utilitarian construct. The premise of the pro-aborts may be utilitarian, but the tactics of the pro-life movement/industry often are as well.

For example, we argue that all life is sacred. Then we seek out legislation that doesn't try to end child killing but seeks to put restrictions on it like waiting periods before killing your kid, but then once the threshold is met a mom can still kill her baby. As pro-life champion and former California Congressman Bob Dornan once said, "If it ends with 'and then you can kill the baby' it's not a pro-life bill."

Another example would be so-called "fetal pain bills." These well-intentioned bills are based on Supreme Court precedent dealing with when the fetus feels pain. First of all, why pro-lifers would use the language of the child killing industry in the first place is beyond me. It's not a fetus, it's a baby. Not to mention these bills basically rely on the reporting of butchers willing to kill babies for a living in order to enforce them. I don't know about you, but if someone (I refuse to refer to them as doctors) is sleeping well at night after dismembering unborn babies for a living, I probably wouldn't trust them too much. Or am I the only one that watches those Lila Rose YouTube videos when she catches Planned Parenthood workers lying all the time?

Remember Kermit Gosnell, the baby butcher of Philadelphia?[63] Sworn testimony in open court during his gruesome trial included witnesses describing one baby born alive as "making this screeching noise" that made it sound "like a little alien" right before Gosnell killed the 18-to-24 inch newborn. Does Gosnell sound like someone you would trust to accurately report prenatal data?

Furthermore, by ending child killing strictly on the basis of when the baby in the womb feels pain, we are not holding the moral high ground of the sanctity of life. Rather, we are surrendering the moral high ground by advancing the utilitarian position

---

63 Steve Deace, "When Foolish Hearts are Darkened," April 11, 2013, http://stevedeace.com/news/national-politics/when-foolish-hearts-are-darkened/

of the quality of life instead. In other words, we're protecting the child on the basis of when it can feel pain, not on the basis of when/if it's actually a child.

Now might be a good time to define utilitarianism, which is a humanist ethic/philosophy based on maximizing pleasure and minimizing pain for the most public and/or individual good. It's a totally subjective standard not based on moral absolutes, but rather what's best for the whims, desires, impulses, and preferences for those wanting to justify their actions. Utilitarianism was a driving philosophical force in the former Soviet Union—"from each according to his abilities, to each according to his needs."

Utilitarianism runs contrary to the "Laws of Nature and Nature's God" referenced in our founding document, which is the fixed standard embedded in the creation by the Creator Himself for our own good, and is so obvious our Founding Fathers called it "self evident."

Utilitarianism allows ethics to evolve based on what individuals or societies prefer or believe is optimal at the time or necessary to drive their materialistic bottom line. Meanwhile the "Laws of Nature and Nature's God" is an objective moral standard that is always what's best for individuals and societies, because it is the very blueprint devised by the loving God in whose image we are all made.

Violating His moral law is just as foolish as violating His laws of physics. For instance, a man may have a great desire to fly. He wants to fly more than anything in the world, but the problem is he doesn't have wings or any other anatomical appendage that lends itself to flying. Still, his desire is to fly. He finds others who share his desires. He hires lawyers to sue for his right to fly, and lobbyists to advocate for laws allowing human flight regardless of what our anatomy allows.

After raising enough of a ruckus, he finally finds a human authority that validates his right to fly. Still, he has no wings. Nevertheless, ruled by nothing other than his own passions, he climbs to the top of the highest building in his hometown. Convinced because of his innate desire to fly that he must have the right to soar through the air, he flings himself off the top of that building.

What happens?

Splat happens. Regardless of how he felt, he still ran smack-dab into the natural law of gravity, which changes for no man. The law of gravity was here long before he got here, and it will be here long after he's gone. The law of gravity is here for our own good, and when we violate that law of gravity there are consequences in order to deter future violations.

There are four symptoms of a society that has abandoned the "Laws of Nature and Nature's God" in exchange for a utilitarian ethic. A utilitarian society will become a culture of the four Ds:

Decadence: Liberty becomes licentiousness, self expression becomes selfishness, and the pursuit of happiness becomes materialism. Moral standards are summed up with phrases like "if it feels good do it" and "as long as you're not hurting anybody else it's ok."

Decay: Traditions and institutions that a society once leaned upon to maintain the proper relationship between the government and the governed, as well as the rule of law, are allowed to deteriorate until they are eventually ignored and cast aside altogether.

Debt: Personal accountability and responsibility are replaced by the common good, which means it becomes the role of society to enable, validate, and in some cases subsidize the individual's quest for self actualization/gratification—provided that individual is an asset and not a liability. Valuable corporate entities that make bad decisions become "too big to fail" and require government bailouts. If someone wants to acquire the education and training necessary to become a productive member of society, then society must pay for it and then society has a claim on the wages that person earns once they're successful. In short, the ends justify the means. The endgame is almost always the creation of a ruling class, or elites, as those in public policy (government) and captains of industry (business) monolithically join together since it's obvious we need them to make all our decisions for us.

Death: Once a person is labeled a liability, discarding them is justified. If unmarried high school sweethearts conceive a child in a hotel room on prom night, that unborn child can be killed because its birth gets in the way of what they have planned with the rest of their lives. With no moral constraints on flawed human nature, resources and revenues grow scarce, so the population must be controlled to manage them. Unproductive workers or minority groups can be purged if it is determined they have outlived their usefulness, and/or become a drain on the system. An elderly woman who is disabled can be tossed aside by the healthcare system in favor of the able-bodied and productive. Schoolchildren are conditioned to adopt this value system through tests which list ten people stranded on a boat that will sink unless four of them are tossed overboard. Students are given the background on all ten passengers, and then select which foursome's lives are worthy of sacrificing with the idea the needs of the many outweigh the needs of the few—or the one.

Does any of this sound familiar? Hits a little too close to home, doesn't it?

The "Laws of Nature and Nature's God" contradicts all of this. It says the Creator doesn't sacrifice the one to save 99, but rather leaves 99 behind to save the one. It says the Creator sacrifices Himself for us to be reconciled with Him, so we should be willing to sacrifice ourselves to be reconciled with one another. It says a husband and father should sacrifice himself for his wife and children, and his wife should sacrifice herself for him while he's doing so. It says we are to be accountable for our actions *and* bear one another's burdens. It says love knows nothing greater than a man willing to lay down his life for his friends. It says ask not what your country can do for you, but ask what you can do for your country.

Like in the movie *Saving Private Ryan*, where Tom Hanks leads a squadron of soldiers who re-enter a combat zone to risk their lives to save just one from their band of brothers. Or in *Schindler's List*, where Oskar Schindler laments at the end he couldn't save them all from the gas chamber rather than slapping himself on the back for the ones he did save.

I have three children, and if all of them fell down a deep well I would do everything I could to get all of them out. If I could only save two, I wouldn't be content and calling myself a hero for only leaving one behind. Instead I would be stricken with grief for the child that was lost, and if I had to I would lay down my life to save all three.

Perhaps the best movie example of what I'm talking about is found in the post-World War II classic *Judgment at Nuremberg*. Burt Lancaster plays a German judge who finds as many loopholes as he can to avoid sending innocent Jews on a one-way trip to the Nazi concentration camps. Sadly, once he runs out of loopholes to exploit, he eventually ends up "following the law" and sentences some innocent Jews to their death. During his trial at Nuremberg, he makes the case that he had no choice but to "follow the law" as a judge, and that he should be considered a hero for doing the best he could. After all, he claims, had someone else more sympathetic to the Nazis been the judge in these cases even more Jews would have died.

Nevertheless, the Allies' prosecutor portrayed by Spencer Tracy successfully convicts him of a death sentence. Why? Because Lancaster's character still violated the "Laws of Nature and Nature's God" which clearly says "do not murder." In the Judeo-Christian moral tradition, that judge is called to uphold the highest law, which is the "Law of Nature and Nature's God," even if it means sacrificing himself. He's not given a helmet sticker for murdering less innocent people. He's not a hero, he's a murderer. A hero risks his life outside a corrupt system to save as many as he can, not play within a corrupt system to kill fewer than someone else would.

That's the difference between the judge in *Judgment at Nuremberg* and the heroic Corrie Ten Boom. One uses the law to hide rather than risking his life for his fellow man. The other risks her life by creating a hiding place for those being persecuted.

I get puffed up press releases whenever a Republican governor or state legislature patronizes us with pro-life license plates, but not nearly as many press releases when Republicans stand in the way of advancing pro-life legislation. Many of us were up in arms about the Obama Regime's contraception mandate on the Catholic Church and its taxpayer funded child killing. But did you know Mitt Romney imposed the exact same mandate on Catholic institutions as governor of Massachusetts with taxpayer-funded child killing as well? I'm sure some folks in the pro-life movement/industry just forgot to Google that one.[64]

In 2006 then President George W. Bush told ABC News[65] he opposed South Dakota's effort to stop child killing in all cases, because it didn't provide for his preferred exceptions for rape, incest, and the life of the mother. In other words, Bush said since pro-lifers were going to stop killing the children he was willing to kill, he'd rather we just kept killing them all.

Did you get an email alert from your favorite pro-life website or organization about that back in the day?

In 2012 I wrote for *Townhall.com* about the former Republican Speaker of the Oklahoma House,[66] who is also a pastor mind you, almost singlehandedly thwarting legislation that would've pro tected life in that state from conception to natural death. Unless you read my column, I doubt you heard about that.

Beyond my Christian moral conviction that all life comes from God and is therefore sacred, as well as my historical recognition of what happens to societies that reject the sanctity of life, I have a personal stake in this fight.

My mother was 14-years old when I was conceived, and 15-years old when she had me. She could've made a choice to move on with the rest of her life, but she chose to protect my life instead. Others in my family meet the criteria of every Republicrat's favorite exceptions (rape, incest, and life of the mother), including two of my own children. My entire family line could have been wiped out by those who claim to be "pro-life with exceptions." So you'll excuse me if I'm a little sensitive to the concept of exceptions for shedding innocent blood. Those exceptions have a name, and more

64 Peter Nicholas, "Romney and Birth Control: A Shift," *Wall Street Journal,* February 13, 2012, http://online.wsj.com/news/articles/SB10001424052970204062704577219564164388218

65 Steven Ertelt, "President Bush Comments on South Dakota Abortion Ban in Interview," *Life News,* March 1, 2006, http://archive.lifenews.com/nat2114.html

66 Steve Deace, "Republicans Nullifying Conservatives," *Townhall,* April 21, 2012, http://townhall.com/columnists/stevedeace/2012/04/21/republicans_nullifying_conservatives

importantly they have an eternal soul and a purpose. Some of those exceptions are people very near and dear to me.

Some of those exceptions are pro-life warriors like Rebecca Kiessling, who was conceived in rape. Kiessling appeared at the screening of a pro-life film in my home state back in 2011, and graciously yet forcefully confronted Texas Governor Rick Perry on his "pro-life with exceptions" stance. She told him, "I'm one of those exceptions. How come others like me don't have a right to live?" Perry was so moved by her testimony that he publicly repented of his position, and a week later appeared on my radio program to talk about the impact Kiessling made on his pro-life moral conviction.

There is no such thing as "pro-life with exceptions." If someone is "pro-life with exceptions" they're really just pro-choice, but just want fewer choices than Planned Parenthood does. For if you really believed we were killing innocent children, you would do everything you could to stop it regardless of the circumstances.

Imagine if a political candidate was "pro not beating your wife with exceptions." In general he thinks beating your wife is wrong, but in very extreme circumstances that only happen 2% of the time he thinks it's either justified or not his place to judge. Would you vote for a wife beater? Or is he not a wife beater because 98% of the time he's opposed to it? If he only beats his own wife during one of those 2% exceptions, do the police not charge him with domestic abuse like they would any other more egregious wife beater?

You cannot prevail in any moral cause if you surrender the moral high ground. For 40 years pro-lifers have surrendered the moral high ground from a sanctity of life *conviction*, to a quality of life *position*. Which to a lesser degree is actually the very utilitarian premise asserted by the child killing industry.

Many pro-lifers were touting a 2012 Gallup Poll that said a majority of Americans considered themselves "pro-life."[67] However,

---

67 Lydia Saad, "Pro-Choice Americans at Record Low," Gallup, May 23, 2012, http://www.gallup.com/poll/154838/pro-choice-americans-record-low.aspx

the devil in that poll was truly in the details. Only 20% of Americans believed in upholding "do not murder" by making child killing via abortion illegal in all circumstances. Might I suggest that if only 20% of Americans are willing to enforce the commandment "do not murder" then there's no way 51% of the American people are pro-life, because they don't know what pro-life is. They might be "pro-er life" than they used to be, or they might think child killing on-demand is icky, but they're not pro-life.

Suppose a majority of folks in your neighborhood told you they were against anyone murdering you, but at the same time only 20% of them were willing to make murdering you illegal regardless of the circumstances. How safe would you feel in that neighborhood? Likewise, about the most dangerous place for an American baby nowadays is tragically inside his mother's womb. We in the pro-life movement are at least somewhat at fault for this, for we have been surrendering the moral high ground on this travesty for decades. A 2013 article in *Time Magazine*[68] did about the best and most honest job of covering the current divide within the pro-life movement I have seen yet.

The schism comes down to two questions:

1. Is *all* life sacred and worthy of protection?
2. What is the strategy to ultimately end the tragedy of child killing in America?

The fact that following the 40th anniversary year of *Roe v. Wade* we still aren't of one mind on the two most important questions of our movement is exactly why the killing continues.

Time points out that there are some claiming to be pro-life that either don't believe all life is sacred and worthy of protection, and/or have no strategy to ultimately end the slaughter of over 50 million children in America the past 40 years.

At the heart of the debate is an emerging group within the

---

68 Grace Wyler, "Personhood Movement Continues to Divide Pro-Life Activists," *Time Magazine*, July 24, 2013, http://nation.time.com/2013/07/24/personhood -movement-continues-to-divide-pro-life-activists/

pro-life movement called Personhood USA, whom I partnered with to put forth a pledge signed by almost every 2012 Republican presidential candidate. Despite the massive influence and size of the pro-life voting bloc within the Republican Party for decades, our pledge was sadly the first to demand potential Republican Party standard-bearers actually uphold the standard that makes us pro-lifers.

The "personhood movement" actually has a plan to end child killing in America once and for all. In fact, it's the only workable plan I know of. That plan is to establish by law that a "person" is a person at the moment of biological beginning under the 5th and 14th Amendments to the U.S. Constitution, which say "no person" shall be "deprived of life, liberty, or property without due process of law."

Isn't this what you believe if you're pro-life?

Personhood USA also believes in the "God-given right to life" and that all persons are "created in the image of God."

Isn't this what you believe if you're pro-life?

The reason Personhood USA's plan is workable is because it comes right from the original *Roe v. Wade* hearing itself.[69] During the hearing several Supreme Court Justices acknowledged that if it could be established the human fetus is a person under the Constitution, the child killing industry would have an almost impossible case to make. To which the attorney advocating child killing before the U.S. Supreme Court responded, "I would have a very difficult case."

It doesn't get any more practical than using your enemy's acknowledged weakness against them.

You're probably wondering why this is so controversial for some within the pro-life movement? After all, isn't this what we claim to believe? As someone that has been involved in these debates within the movement at a high level, I have never gotten a good answer from my Pro-Life brethren who oppose this.

But don't just take my word for it. Look at what they told *Time.*

---

69 http://www.youtube.com/watch?v=81NrWq3p5Ag

The legislative director for Wisconsin Right to Life told *Time* she was "done talking about the Personhood Amendment" currently underway in her state. She went on to say, "This particular measure might sound good from a pro-life perspective, but it's not going to save one single life."

So apparently following the very blueprint the Supreme Court gave us to defeat *Roe v. Wade* in the actual hearing "won't save a single life?" Establishing by law that a "person" is a person at the moment of biological beginning using language right out of the U.S. Constitution won't "save a single life?" I fail to understand that logic. Maybe one of you reading this book can educate me?

Is there an explanation for this? I've tried to get answers. I even went directly to the head of my National Right to Life chapter in my home state of Iowa. My pastor served on her board of directors at the time, and even then she couldn't give me a single good reason why they still have never helped us with establishing personhood in our state legislature. I still have the emails from those conversations. Her lack of good answers is why my pastor no longer serves on the board of Iowa Right to Life.

This lack of push for personhood from some notable sectors of the Pro-Life movement is one of the major reasons why personhood initiatives have failed in several states so far. Of course, abolition of slavery failed at first several times as well, but ultimately succeeded by never surrendering the moral high ground. Personhood USA hopes to emulate that historical success.

If my fellow Pro-Lifers don't believe "personhood" is the right strategy to ultimately end child killing in America, then what is theirs? If the strategy is we just wait for *Roe v. Wade* to be overturned, don't we need an offensive initiative to force that question before the court? Isn't the question of who is or isn't a person that very offensive initiative?

It seems to me the only argument we have against abortion is that we're killing persons. Elsewhere we agree with arguments that say the government has no role in telling you what to do with your own body or conscience. Don't we oppose things like the Obamacare mandate on similar grounds? The only reason we don't accept that language in the case of abortion is it's not your body, but rather somebody else's. If it's not a person, there's no reason to oppose abortion. Therefore, it would only seem logical to me that's the debate we want to have.

In 2013 the Media Research Center visited a college campus to get students to sign a petition in favor of "4th trimester abortions."[70] Their lack of critical thinking displayed by the fact they didn't recognize the self-refuting logic of the petition itself (there can never be a 4th tri-mester), several students bought all the same pro-child killing talking points for killing already-born babies. And they were willing to say so on camera. It seems to me that if folks aren't even aware of when pregnancy ends they sure don't know when life begins. And if folks don't know when life begins, they don't when they're obligated to protect life.

Or as President Obama once flippantly told Pastor Rick Warren when he asked him the question of when life begins, "That's above my paygrade."

But while some notable sectors of the Pro-Life movement refuse to sign on, personhood is gaining ground in Washington, D.C. of all places. *Time* says former Republican vice presidential candidate Paul Ryan has introduced a personhood bill that has 38 co-sponsors in the House of Representatives, and Senator Rand Paul has introduced similar legislation in the U.S. Senate. Potential 2016 GOP presidential candidates Marco Rubio and Scott Walker are also supporters of personhood, according to *Time*.

Yet despite that momentum, *Time* says "mainstream anti-abortion groups like Americans United for Life and Susan B. Anthony List have distanced themselves from the personhood movement."

So instead of defending life at conception without exceptions, what are they doing instead? Get this, *Time* says they are "adopting the rhetoric of women's health used by their pro-choice counterparts" so that they can target "the 52% of Americans who think abortion should be legal in some, but not all, cases."

---

70 Steve Deace, "Are You for 4th Trimester Abortions?" August 14, 2013, http://stevedeace.com/news/national-politics/are-you-for-4th-trimester-abortions/

In other words, according to *Time* neither Americans United for Life nor Susan B. Anthony List is actively standing for the God-given right to life. Just because you're anti-abortion doesn't mean you're pro-life.

Fellow pro-lifer, did you get into this fight so that killing children would be "legal in some, but not all, cases?" Do you think there is ever a good reason to kill an innocent child? Do you think we should execute children for the crimes of their parents? If you believe all of us are made in the image of God, does that same God ever provide exceptions for the shedding of innocent blood?

The head of Americans United for Life tells *Time* she doesn't believe as you do. She says "the pro-life movement is not one size fits all. We're the ones occupying the middle ground."

It would seem to me asserting the God-given right to life is "one size fits all." Either you have a right to life or you don't. It's not as if only two-thirds (or shall we say three-fifths) of you can be alive and the rest dead.

Furthermore, what is "the middle ground" of a dead, innocent child? Since we've killed more than 50 million children in the past 40 years, is "the middle ground" killing only 25 million? So if we only killed 25 million would killing children be any less evil? What if we only killed one million?

Can you find "the middle ground" with those who chant "Hail Satan" and throw feces and tampons to defend their blood lust, like we saw at the Texas State Legislature in 2013?

The child killing industry understands there is no middle ground. You're either for killing children or you're not. This is why they fight so vehemently against even commonsense restrictions to prevent more Kermit Gosnells. They understand the antidote to their plague on our land is establishing the personhood of every American—from the moment of biological beginning *without exceptions.*

"The bottom line is that (Personhood USA) is trying to end all abortion once and for all," the litigation director for the Center of Reproductive Rights told *Time.*

She's exactly right. That is what we're trying to do.

Fellow Pro-Lifer, isn't that what you want to do? Don't you want to end child killing once and for all? Are you giving your time, talent, and treasure to a group that shares your conviction?

Meanwhile, the killing continues.

This is why I am a strong supporter of groups like Personhood USA.

The "personhood movement" is based on four things:

1. The belief that all life comes from God and thus is sacred from the moment of conception with no exceptions. Therefore, a person is defined as such from biological beginning to natural death.

2. The highest law is the "Law of Nature and Nature's God," and that law commands "do not murder." Therefore, any edicts or decrees from any human authority, including the Supreme Court, that contradict that highest law are unjust and should be challenged to the point of civil disobedience if necessary.

3. The 5th and 14th Amendments to the U.S. Constitution say that no "person" shall be denied "life or property without due process of law." Since unborn children are persons and have not been given due process, then the government has a moral obligation to protect their inalienable right to life as it would any other person.

4. Personhood is referred to in the *Roe v. Wade* opinion itself when Justice Harry Blackmun writes, "If this suggestion of personhood is established, the appellant's case, of course, collapses, for the fetus' right to life would then be guaranteed specifically by the (5th) Amendment." The prenatal technology we have available today is light years more advanced than what was available in 1973 at the time of *Roe v. Wade*. If you have ever seen your own child *in utero* via modern prenatal technology, then you know that is not an "unviable tissue mass" you are looking at, but your baby.

Personhood is the principled and proper expression of the sanctity of life, because it retakes the moral high ground. Instead of debating with one another how many we're willing to continue to kill, it forces the opposition to define why it doesn't believe all should be allowed to live. Instead of attacking the *practice* of killing children it attacks the *premise* for it.

The civil rights movement correctly believed that inequality for some meant inequality for all. The pro-life movement will not experience victory until it draws the same line in the sand, and it has its predecessor the abolitionist movement to look to as an example.

Originally there were attempts to regulate slavery incrementally in an effort to both isolate it and prohibit its expansion. After decades of failure, the anti-slavery movement came to the conclusion that it was abolition or nothing. As renowned 19th century abolitionist William Lloyd Garrison put it, "Enslave the liberty of but one man and the liberties of the world are put in peril."

Now *that* is capturing the moral high ground, and that is how you prevail in a moral cause. Whether it's the sanctity of life, the definition of marriage, the rule of law, or the integrity of our currency and banking system, these issues are all moral enterprises.

There can be no compromise when it comes to moral enterprises; compromise is defeat. How do you compromise on moral enterprises such as life anyways? Is the baby less dead?

From the Puritans to the patriots, this republic was founded by those who refused to surrender the moral high ground, and it will only be preserved if we resolve to do the same.

6

Reverse the Premise of Your Opponent's Argument, and Use it Against Him

How many times have you watched the presidential debates in the post-Reagan years with your hands half-covering your eyes, just dreading that moment when that gotcha question comes "our guy's" way?

You can almost sense it coming too, can't you? Just when "our guy" seems to have the momentum and a head of steam, you know the liberal media member pretending to be an impartial moderator is going to drop the proverbial hammer right on our heads.

Come on, I can't be the only grassroots conservative out there who has experienced this level of angst watching these things? Be honest with me now. Don't leave me hanging. That's what I thought.

I mean, heaven forbid our Republican "champion" actually has the worldview and shrewd communication skills to turn the question to his advantage. I mean, we're only running for the highest offices in the land here, so it's not like we should expect the best of the best to represent us or anything.

At this point our expectations are so low we'd settle for our Republican "champion" to just stop ceding even more ground to the Left, let alone taking some back. Too often while watching the campaigns of establishment candidates "our guy" actually tries to get to the left of the questioner instead of standing up to him.

For instance, you knew the 2008 campaign was over when John McCain mavericked himself all the way to the left of Barack Obama during the bailout, even going so far in one presidential debate as to call for the taxpayers to buy off all the bad home loan debt on top of the TARP.

I'm guessing I wasn't the only conservative who was throwing things and screaming words a Christian man should never say at the television screen as Obama got to scold McCain for demanding too much from the taxpayers on national television.

We've already written about not accepting the premise of your opponent, but the next step to winning requires borrowing a technique from the martial arts—using your opponent's strength against him. In political combat we do that by first rejecting your opponent's premise, and then we reverse his premise and use it against him.

Or, as Shakespeare put it in *Hamlet*, to "hoist him from his own petard."

Reagan was a Jedi Master of this technique, and here are just a couple of many famous examples.

During a 1984 presidential debate with Walter Mondale, Reagan responded to mounting criticism he was too old to be president by promising he would not "make his opponent's youth and inexperience an issue in this campaign."

That snarky retort even drew a laugh from Mondale himself.

At a press conference during his first term, ABC News' Chief White House Correspondent Sam Donaldson asked Reagan if all the blame for the recession at the time rested with the Democrat-controlled Congress. "Mr. President, does any of the blame belong to you," Donaldson asked Reagan.

Without skipping a beat, Reagan winsomely replied, "Yes, because for many years I was a Democrat."

While there may never be another Reagan (but Texas Senator Ted Cruz looks like the closest thing we've had since), there is no reason why we can't do a better job of hoisting the opposition from its own petard. But to do so requires some of that 3-D thinking I referred to in the introduction.

You cannot successfully reverse your opponent's premise if you accept it, and unless you know why you believe what you believe you will accept your opponent's premise more times than not. In the first Reagan example we just cited, notice he rejects the premise outright that he's too old for the job. So instead of arguing his qualifications, he makes a crack undercutting the qualifications of his opponent.

"But Steve," some of you will say, "aren't we tired of politicians who won't answer the question they were asked?"

Yes, but if the premise of the question is flawed you should never dignify it with an answer. Gotcha questions with no attempt to address anything substantive are the Left's version of "did you beat your wife last night?" Once you start going down that rabbit trail, you end up chasing your own tail. Instead, you need to reverse the premise and put them on the defensive.

Let them know that it ain't no fun when the rabbit's got the gun.

On the other hand, you also don't want to come across as evasive, which is why reversing the premise and using it against them is so key. You're turning the argument of your opponent around on them to demonstrate the total lack of substance and merit of their argument.

In the second aforementioned Reagan example, he utilizes the second dimension of our 3-D thinking perfectly, which is know why others believe what they believe. Reagan knew that Donaldson was a liberal. Therefore, Reagan knew what Donaldson was looking for. Donaldson wasn't looking for a substantive discussion on what policies were necessary to get us out of the recession at the time. Donaldson was trying to get Reagan to use his bully pulpit to admit the recession he inherited from Jimmy Carter was his fault. This was a pure gotcha question.

That knowledge helped Reagan respond by taking Donaldson's premise and strangling him with it. Essentially Reagan said, "Fine, Sam. You want me to accept blame for what big government does to stifle capitalism and free enterprise? Sure, I should probably accept some of that blame for all the years I used to be a big government Democrat advocating these same failed policies myself."

That, my friends, is what the kids today refer to as a walk-off shot or a mic drop.

It's as automatic as Mariano Rivera coming out of the bullpen for the New York Yankees in the ninth inning to close the game. The crowd knows it's safe to head out early and get the jump on the Bronx zoo on the way home. Good night and drive home safely.

Unfortunately, most of my fellow grassroots patriots reading this are painfully aware we have so few potential champions today capable of duplicating these examples. In a sound-bite driven society like ours, the ability to be pithy and potent while trying to persuade others to your principles is pivotal. Folks don't give you 30 minutes to make your case today. They give you 30 seconds.

Since we communicate in such a quick-draw style nowadays, it is imperative that we are quick-on-the-draw in the arena of ideas. Whether it's a grassroots patriot standing up to speak at a local Tea Party rally, one of our elected officials or candidates on a national stage, or just a conversation about politics between you and your neighbor, if you can't instantly grab people's attention and make your case they just move on.

People are used to getting their news from Drudge's compilation of headlines, and often don't read the actual articles linked, or don't read beyond the first couple of paragraphs if they do. Instead of letters we communicate with our family via Facebook status updates, and with our friends in 140 characters or less on Twitter.

Furthermore, the other side of the debate has already boiled down their positions to emotion-driven clichés that are easy to embed into the subconscious of our fellow Americans (e.g. marriage equality, a woman's right to choose, government investment, income equality, fairness, diversity, standing up for the middle class, etc.) It's easier to communicate emotion in a pithy fashion than it is logic and reason, which is often what we base our positions on, so we're already at a disadvantage. That's why we need to be intentional about equipping one another to communicate in a way that resonates with how most of our fellow Americans receive and distribute information.

One of the most effective methods of doing just that is to master the art of reversing the premise of our opponent's argument and using it against them. Let me provide a couple more examples from my own experience.

I once did a TV interview where I sat in a chair and the host had three minutes to ask me anything he wanted to. This reoccurring segment was designed to put newsmakers on the defensive by forcing them to answer awkward or in-your-face questions off-the-cuff. I figured since I get to do this to newsmakers all the time, it's only fair I put myself on the hot seat for a change. Since I'm not shy about airing my worldview, the host was aware of my socially conservative views, so he went for the jugular right away.

"Do you have any gay family members or friends," he asked.

Now this is the kind of question that normally makes us cringe after one of our so-called "champions" is asked something like this by the liberal media. The premise of the question is that people determine the moral standard, and not the moral standard (the "Law of Nature and Nature's God") itself. So if I have family members and friends who are same-sex attracted and I live and let live with them, why don't I do this for others? After all, what's wrong with two people loving each other, right?

Except I never accepted the premise of his question, and instead turned it around on him.

"All of my friends and everyone in my family are either male or female," I said.

He looked puzzled and repeated his question.

"Everybody I know is male or female," I repeated. "I'm not aware of a third variation of the human species, but if you've discovered one I'd get the patent on that research quick-like, because I'm guessing there's some money to be made there."

It was clear he'd never run into anybody capable of doing this before, and was used to framing the argument. Left with no liberal clichés to rely upon, he had to just come right out and say it.

"Is anybody you know or care about currently having sex with someone of the same gender," he awkwardly asked.

First, by never accepting his premise I have forced him to accept mine, which is our gender is pre-determined at birth no matter what our desires and preferences are. Therefore gender identity and sexual orientation are really just Orwellian talking points devised to distract us from what we're really talking about here—who someone wants to have sex with and how they want to have sex with them.

This isn't about any virtue higher than men having sex with men and women having sex with women, despite the fact the anatomy of each makes that rather difficult on its own because the parts weren't designed to work that way.

In addition, by making him ask his question this way, it looks like he's the one on a witch hunt and not me. Most Americans, regardless of political persuasion, have wrongly privatized sexual ethics. I heard from several people who saw the interview how they couldn't believe he was butting his nose into my private business like that. While I don't agree with that premise, I'm certainly more than willing to reverse it and use it against him, and when I did so I went in for the kill.

"I don't make it a habit of calling my friends and family members and asking them who they had sex with last night," I said, as if their private sexual behavior was none of my business.

Like Bill Paxton said in the movie *Aliens*, "Game over man!"

The entire faulty premise of the homosexual agenda is that what two consenting adults are doing in their bedroom is of no business to anybody else. In reality the motto of this movement is "you will be made to care." That's why they make it our business by invading the public policy arena demanding validation for their private bedroom behavior in a manner that compels the rest of us to alter our morality and religious freedom to accommodate them. By forcing the interviewer to pester me to the point he had no choice but to abandon the liberal talking points and invade my family's privacy, I had reversed his faulty premise and used it against him. Even better, this all happened in less than 90 seconds so it kept everyone's attention.

After the interview, Dick Bott of Bott Radio Network, a legend in Christian broadcasting, called me to tell me that was about the best defense of "our belief system" in three minutes he'd ever seen.

I was faced with a similar situation on another issue during a nationally-televised interview I did during the 2012 presidential primary. I was challenged by the interviewer with how I, as a Christian, could talk about grace and love while at the same time argue to end government programs to help the poor and needy?

Again, this is the sort of question that all too often the Mitt McCains and George McDoles face from the national media that produces a cringe-inducing response. But if you have a solid worldview, it's like sitting on a fastball with a 3-1 count.

"I think grace and love are measured in a culture not by how many people are in need of government assistance but by how many people no longer do," I said. "What can be more loving than encouraging your fellow man created in the image of God that with the right training, tools, and opportunity they can rise above their circumstances and fulfill their God-given potential?"

There was no follow up question after that.

If the welfare state really meant compassion, then how come Democrats aren't bragging about the fact there are currently more Americans on food stamps than the population of Spain?[71] Shouldn't they be thanking the taxpayers for all this "compassion?" Shouldn't they be holding press junkets to boast their plan is working, and we're the most compassionate society we've ever been?

Instead of screaming, swearing, and throwing things at the TV screen while Republicrats roll over and play dead for the liberal media, we'd be standing and applauding if more conservatives in the spotlight said things like that more often. Remember when

---

71 Elizabeth Harrington, "Food Stamp Rolls in America Now Surpass the Population of Spain," CNS News, February 11, 2013, http://cnsnews.com/news/article/food -stamp-rolls-america-now-surpass-population-spain

Newt Gingrich got a standing ovation at the 2012 South Carolina primary debate when he turned the tables just like that on Fox News' Juan Williams?

One of the most devastating ways to deploy premise reversal is with the use of humor, especially of the snarky variety. I will often use stories going viral as an opportunity to hoist the Left from its own petard. Case in point is the strange tale of Raymond Foley.[72]

The 59-year old Foley was charged with "chair wetting." After hours at work he was urinating on the chairs of the women he found attractive. In response to this story, I opened my show one night with this monologue:

> *Raymond Foley is a victim.*
>
> *Sure, in past eras far less enlightened and tolerant as this current gilded age, Foley might be considered a menace to society—a creep even. But we know better now. We know people just can't control their urges, and to demand otherwise is a Neanderthal concept right out of the stone (tablet) age.*
>
> *Foley was born with something that compels him to act out in ways some segments of our society still clinging to their guns and religion condemn. But what Foley doesn't need is judgment. Foley needs understanding.*
>
> *Foley, 59, was recently charged with second degree mischief for simply being who he is. Who is Foley?*
>
> *Foley is a chair-wetter.*
>
> *According to police in Iowa, Foley was looking up his fellow female employees in the Farm Bureau company database. If he found the woman attractive he would then go to her desk after hours and urinate on her empty chair.*
>
> *For months several female employees were complaining about a strange scent emanating from their chairs. Eventually it was discovered the smell was that of urine, and the urine was Foley's.*
>
> *Once forced to come out of the closet, Foley clearly felt like the*

---

72 Steve Deace, "Urination Orientation," *Townhall*, April 7, 2012, http://townhall.com/columnists/stevedeace/2012/04/07/urination_orientation/page/full

COMMANDMENT #5 | 121

weight of the world had been lifted off his shoulders because he voluntarily surrendered to police. No longer having to hide who he is, Foley is willing to accept responsibility for his admittedly odd actions. We can only hope that Foley will simultaneously seek to raise awareness of them as well.

That's because Foley is just the most high-profile example of the latest progressive form of self expression. Foley, like an increasing number of Americans, has discovered he has a urination orientation.

Shamed by society, folks like Foley have been forced to act on their urges in the shadows. Whether it's urinating on empty chairs or perhaps over-indulging their senses via depictions of urination on adult websites, Foley and others like him are being denied their right to urinate.

It is, after all, the way they were made. All of us have the desire to urinate. It's part of our base nature. But where does someone else get off (so to speak) telling someone else what form that urination must take? Or even where that urination must take place?

Laws that deny public expression of urination are just another example of the government regulating what we do with our own bodies. Until these laws are repealed, and people like Foley affirmed their right to urinate on whichever consenting adult or inanimate object they choose, none of us can trust our rights will be defended. For if one group is denied their freedom then it's just a matter of time before "straight shooters"—slang for those who prefer to uri-nate into toilets (or on them, depending on their aim)—will also be threatened.

Some of you are sure to be offended by what Foley has done, but how dare you judge Foley until you've walked a mile in his shoes (or spent some time in his chair). Besides, someone cannot change the way they were born thus it's not right to shun Foley simply for acting on his nature. The chairs were empty, remember, and surely the urine dried by the time the women returned to work the next morning. Foley wasn't doing anything that harmed anybody else, and it's not like you can spread some disease via airborne urine.

If that reasoned argument doesn't persuade you then answer this simple question: how has Foley being able to act on his urination orientation negatively impacted your urination? If it hasn't impeded your "stream" of consciousness then what Foley is doing is none of your business and you should urinate when and where you choose and permit Foley to do the same.

Granted, the chairs Foley was urinating on were someone else's property, but that's simply because neither his employer nor the government provided the means by which Foley could properly apply his urination orientation. If Foley had access to chairs pretty girls once sat on to urinate in, he wouldn't have to urinate on the chairs he actually did. That's not even addressing the fact that if the government doesn't provide Foley chairs to urinate in, he'll continue doing it after hours in chairs that could be faulty. Faulty chairs may collapse, thus putting Foley in jeopardy. We don't want people being harmed by collapsing chairs in back hallways do we?

That's exactly why the state ought to be providing those chairs for Foley and others like him. It could potentially save lives, not to mention some chairs (which is good for the environment). Then the state should make sure the next generation of kids in our schools doesn't succumb to the same intolerance and lack of diversity towards urination orientation that their fundamentalist parents and grandparents have victimized folks like Foley with.

Furthermore, the company Foley used to work for should not only give him his job back, but also provide employees such as Foley "urination stations" to be utilized when the urge strikes. Of course adding language to the company diversity curriculum informing Foley's co-workers of the vital necessity of recognizing urination orientation in the workplace, and the important contributions to society urinators have made throughout human history (think of how many important people in history have been bed-wetters, for example), should be immediate actions any good corporate citizen would immediately agree to.

Given the fact a company like Farm Bureau would prefer to avoid looking like an agent of intolerance in the media, I'm confident it will do exactly that.

Some of you reading this will bristle at recognizing both the normalcy and necessity of people like Foley being affirmed and

*accepted for just being who they are, but many of you also bristled
at things 20 years ago you're readily accepting now (or at least tired
of fighting over).*

*Nevertheless, even if those questioning or struggling with their
urination orientation aren't accepted by your generation, rest assured
they will be by your children once we're through enlightening them.
Soon you will see more urination in your classrooms, and all of the
best and most likeable characters on your most popular television
shows will urinate freely on-screen. We'll even have clergy arguing
that the Bible affirms urination in all its forms.*

*And we'll have a pioneer like Foley to thank for it. Who knows?
Maybe Sean Penn will even play the part of Foley in his biopic one
day?*

D.L. Moody once said, "When you're winsome you win some."
In addition, there's an old saying which goes "what the devil hates
most of all is to be mocked." In one of my all-time favorite movies,
Star Trek II: The Wrath of Khan, Captain Kirk gets his nemesis
Khan to lose his cool and manipulates him into a trap by saying,
"Khan, I'm laughing at (your) superior intellect."

Making fun of the foolishness of the Left's magical thinking by
using their own premises against them wins people over to our
side and diminishes their credibility. Beyond the obvious double-
standard that exists, one of the reasons why liberal comedians get
away with being more vicious than conservative commentators is
because people find them funny. People let you absolutely annihilate your opponent if you make them laugh while you're doing it.

What I have learned doing talk radio is that when I only go
after our opponents using harsh language I can at times offend
even those who agree with me. But if I use humor almost everybody gives me permission to be vicious, provided it's funny. If you
make them laugh it's almost as if the public gives you permission
to swing away.

But to be able to use humor and snark that effectively requires
an inner joy, and that inner joy comes only from a deep, abiding
faith that, no matter what, God is still on the throne. The more I've

grown in my faith, the more I believe my heavenly daddy can beat up their earthly daddy. The more I believe my daddy can beat up their daddy, the more peace I have about the future. The more peace I have about the future, the easier it is for me to relax and not always react emotionally. The easier it is for me to relax and not always react emotionally, the easier it is for me to find the humor (joy) in all but the most tragic of circumstances. And the more I can use humor to make my point, the more likely I will get my point across.

People ask me all the time how it seems we're having so much fun chronicling the fall of Western Civilization on the radio. I take that question as a compliment.

Proving the emperor has no clothes doesn't just defeat your enemies, it de-pants them. The reason men like William F. Buckley, C.S. Lewis, and G.K. Chesterton are so often quoted is because they had the wisdom *and* wit to rhetorically remove their opponent's still-beating heart from his chest and show it to everybody with one skillful turn of a phrase.

That doesn't mean there's not a time and place for passion and/ or righteous indignation. Heck, I could probably title my radio program "Righteous Indignation" some nights. I come to work each night with a jawbone of an ass and whip of cords ready to go. But if I really believe in the God of providence expressed in the final verse of our national anthem, there's no reason to be so uptight and antsy all the time.

Incessant hand-wringing is not a heavenly virtue. Besides, if folks don't want to do what's right, the eternal accountability they'll face from God is far more lethal and terrifying than anything I have the power to devise this side of eternity anyway. Just kick the dust off your sandals/cowboy boots and move on.

By all means never stop clinging to your guns and your Bibles, but there's no need to do so bitterly.

Let's engage in one more exercise in reversing the premise, and use the hot-button issue of illegal immigration to do it.

In a clear attempt to pander for Hispanic votes during the 2012 presidential campaign, President Obama unilaterally enacted amnesty for illegals by refusing to enforce the law (see that as violate his oath of office) in cases involving 880,000 illegal aliens (notice I didn't accept the premise they're undocumented immigrants anymore than a car-jacking is an "undocumented repossession"). One of the arguments frequently used by amnesty advocates like Obama, and even some misguided Christian leaders who don't have a theological leg to stand on by agreeing with him, was that it's not fair to penalize children for the mistakes of their parents.

Except if this was really and only about fairness and not punishing kids for the mistakes of their parents, then why do we have borders at all? There are plenty of children suffering throughout the world for circumstances they had nothing to do with, so why don't we bring all of them here and give them access to the welfare state (see that as your productivity and prosperity)?

Why is it fair for middle class Americans to buy a 70 inch television set with so much suffering in the world? Shouldn't the government cap television purchases at 42-inches and redistribute the rest of the wealth to fight global poverty? Come to think of it, who really even needs a 42-inch television set, or television at all for that matter?

Is it fair that First Lady Michelle Obama wore a $1,000 skirt on a trip to Hawaii in 2011? Shouldn't she have bought a cheaper skirt at Wal-Mart, and given the rest of the money to Feed the Children, which says $1 dollar per day feeds 8 hungry children in the United States. How many children starved because Mrs. Obama spent $1,000 on a skirt instead of $24.99?

During the 2013 government "shutdown" (and how can something be "shut down" when it's still operating at 83% capacity), we learned when many of them were furloughed that Michelle Obama had a record number of paid staff for a first lady.[73] Did Michelle Obama really need two dozen taxpayer-paid staff members, when as recently as Mamie Eisenhower the First Lady had to pay for her lone assistant out of her own pocket?[74] How many

---

73 http://www.conservativeactionalerts.com/2011/07/michelle-o-and-her-26-servants/

74 Drew Zahn, "Michelle Obama Has Staff of 22 Assistants," *World Net Daily*, August 4, 2009, http://www.wnd.com/2009/08/105957/

illegals have to remain "living in the shadows" so that Michelle Obama can get her nails done?

And while we're at it, why is it fair to cap the "fairness" at kids whose parents successfully arrived here illegally? Where do we get off not providing "fairness" to the children of parents who haven't been able to illegally and successfully cross our borders? Not to mention, what about all the Latinos (and other minorities) currently waiting in line to immigrate to this country legally? Why is it fair to bypass all of them?

In less than a few hundred words I was able to pose several easily understandable questions that reverse the liberals' premise and use it against them, including citing three examples of their own politicians to reinforce my point. What is more likely to persuade our fellow Americans to our side? The tactics I am suggesting or the boring and contrived talking points "our guys" usually regurgitate over and over again to the already-converted on Fox News?

Humor can even be used to reverse the Left's premise on an issue as divisive and potentially hostile as the debate over the definition of marriage. In 2013 I wrote a column for *USA Today*[75] attacking those for redefining marriage as being hypocrites:

> *Those arguing for "marriage equality" at the U.S. Supreme Court this week should be ashamed of themselves.*
>
> *They're just as guilty of discrimination as those dastardly conservatives still bitterly clinging to their guns and their religion. Why no argument for polygamy, polyamory, and other forms of diversity? Why are they only defending their exclusive definition of diversity?*
>
> *How dare those seeking to overturn the Defense of Marriage Act signed by President Clinton, or Proposition 8 ratified by the people of California, stop at just redefining marriage to include two consenting adults of the same gender. Why do these people believe they have the authority to draw a moralistic line against any consenting adults, and thus force their moral standard upon the rest of us?*

---

75 Steve Deace, "A Modest Proposal for Polygamy," *USA Today*, March 30, 2013, http://www.usatoday.com/story/opinion/2013/03/30/gay-marriage-equality/2028619/

Besides, society's views on these other progressive forms of relationship diversity are shifting, and shouldn't we always base our concept of right and wrong off what we see on TV, just like our gender-neutral maternal units taught us. Who better to consult on moral matters than the huddled masses that paid money to see all those Saw and Hostel movies? For example, there is a popular reality show on basic cable called Sister Wives about the lost art of polygamy. Showtime is airing a trailblazing show on the multiple wedded bliss of polyamory.

Oh, sure, Showtime also features a series with a creepy old dude watching 1970s porn with Z-list celebrities as well, but who are we to judge?

Why would those seeking to redefine marriage to include homosexual monogamy play right into the hands of those Draconian religious fundamentalists who think they and their alleged "God" have the authority to narrowly define love among consenting adults? Why aren't those arguing for "marriage equality" being inclusive by including marriage among multiple consenting adults as well? Besides, polygamy is in the Bible no less. Abraham, David and Solomon are just some of that dusty old book's heroes who were polygamists. No member of the American Taliban can claim their puny God destroyed a whole city over polygamy, so why not be more inclusive?

If the government has no power to discriminate against relationships involving two consenting adults of the same gender, then why does it have the power to discriminate against multiple consenting adults of any gender? Next thing you know we'll be back to banning interracial dating!

If we're truly champions of diversity, it's time to embrace polygamy, polyamory, or "multiple marriage." What better way for children to learn about different cultures and belief systems than to grow up around them in their own families. Imagine children being born into a household where each dad has a different religion, each mom speaks a different language and then sometimes the dads are attracted to one another as well as the moms (and vice versa). Talk about covering all your bases! What a richness of blessed diversity could be found in such an endeavor?

It's time for the marriage equality movement to stop being hyp-ocrites and cease practicing its own form of discrimination, and to stop compromising with pro-marriage bigots. Take a principled stand. Either all of us get to do whatever we want with as many whomevers as we want or none of us are equal.

Reversing the premise of the Left's arguments like this and using it against them is one of the most effective and devastating ways to make our point, but to pull it off we need to be confident of our principles and have the required courage of conviction.

Something that is sorely lacking in most of "our guys."

7

Never Abandon Your Base
(unless they're morally wrong)

The only political party in America that despises conservatives and Libertarians more than the Democrats is the Republicans.

That's right, I said it. That just happened. I went there. Fellow patriot, you know this to be true, you just don't want to admit it to yourself. I don't blame you. For several years I didn't want to admit it to myself, either. It's in our nature not to readily accept such inconvenient truths until we come face-to-face with them.

But after years of being stabbed in the back by the leadership of the Republican Party, I am reminded of the words of Thomas Jefferson: "If I could only go to heaven with members of a political party, I would rather not go at all."

In 2008 I watched Mitt Romney spend millions of dollars trying to define Mike Huckabee as some sort of 1970s-style West German Christian Socialist. Then I watched his minions spend $15-20 million trying to destroy Newt Gingrich in the 2012 Florida Primary, even claiming that Gingrich was anti-Reagan during the 1980s despite the fact Michael Reagan, the former president's son, had endorsed Gingrich for president.

This from the man who in 1992 voted for Paul Tsongas in a Democrat primary and in 1994 ran for U.S. Senate against Teddy "splash" Kennedy in opposition to Reagan-Bush. This charade prompted Sarah Palin to respond on her Facebook wall with a note titled "Cannibals in GOP Establishment Deploy Tactics of the Left."

Yet during the 2012 general election campaign, Romney was silent when President Obama came out against marriage after the North Carolina primary, never went to Wisconsin to help Scott Walker during his recall, and punted on making an issue out of the "Fast and Furious" gun-running scandal that led to the deaths of American citizens from weapons the Obama Regime funneled to drug cartels and illegal aliens. Romney even remained mum on "Fast and Furious" after the White House nefariously claimed "executive privilege" rather than demand its Attorney General Eric Holder turn over to Congress documentation about the scandal.

You can bet your sweet bippy that if the Democrat nominee for president was challenging a Republican incumbent under such suspicion, he and the entire liberal media would be calling for impeachment proceedings, let alone the havoc they'd wreak on the campaign trail with it.

But as is typical of the Republican Party establishment, Romney was more willing to go after conservatives in his own party in the primary than he was the Democrats in the general election, which we've seen time and time again. We saw John McCain in 2008 lecture us repeatedly to accept amnesty, and then scold conservatives for referring to his general election campaign rival by his real name—Barack Hussein Obama. Remember in his 2000 campaign when McCain referred to Christians who opposed his then-stance in favor of maintaining *Roe v. Wade* as "agents of intolerance?" McCain can hug Obama, and then shank us. As my friend Daniel Horowitz at the Madison Project once said, "It's tough to confront the enemy with a gun to your head while you've got a knife stuck in your back."

Almost as if he was channeling the misguided maverick, one of Romney's top campaign aides, Eric "etch-a-sketch" Fehnstrom,[76] referred to Christians who believe in the Bible's teaching about homosexuality as "voices of intolerance" within the Republican Party.[77]

Somebody should've asked Fehnstrom if those "voices of intolerance" within the Republican Party include Romney's own Mormon Church, which helped bankroll the Proposition 8 effort to save marriage in California and teaches that all sexual relations outside of a lawfully married man and woman are sinful?

With "friends" like that, who needs liberals, right?

Former Florida Congressman Joe Scarborough, now a television personality on MSNBC, went on an anti-conservative rant on the network[78] telling conservatives to "stay in your mother's basement" and "eat your Cheetos."

"You know, you can go online and act like a jackass and say what you want to say and now everybody is calling Jeb Bush a RINO (Republican in name only). Just shut the hell up. You can stay in your mother's basement. You can eat your Cheetos. You can type on your dingy laptop. That's all you got, but you are not the future of the Republican Party. So just keep screaming at your walls downstairs, your day is done."

By the way, why were conservatives calling Jeb Bush a RINO? Because he was telling us to sellout our cherished principles more, just like his father did when he violated his "read my lips, no new taxes" pledge after becoming president. If I recall, his father lost his next election after doing so. Because in 2013 Jeb Bush was giving

76 Devin Dwyer, "Romney Aide Suggests Campaign Reset After Primary," ABC News, March 21, 2012, http://abcnews.go.com/blogs/politics/2012/03/etch-a-sketch-romney-aide-suggests-campaign-reset-after-primary/

77 Luke Johnson, "Mitt Romney Top Adviser: 'Voices of Intolerance' Led to Richard Grenell Resignation," Huffington Post, May 4, 2012, http://www.huffingtonpost.com/2012/05/04/mitt-romney-richard-grenell-resignation_n_1477163.html

78 Alex Alvarez, "Joe Scarborough to Those Calling Jeb Bush a RINO: You're Not the Future of the GOP," Mediaite, June 12, 2012, http://www.mediaite.com/tv/joe-scarborough-to-those-calling-jeb-bush-a-rino-just-shut-the-hell-up-youre-not-future-of-the-gop/

Hillary "I still have no idea what Benghazi is" Clinton a liberty medal for goodness sake.[79]

Every time we follow the advice of the Jeb Bushes and Joe Scarboroughs of the world, we lose. I mean who doesn't remember the Dole presidency, or Presidents McCain and Romney? Good times.

Not to mention the fact Scarborough has a daily show on national television. Do you ever recall him ranting about Obamacare, Fast and Furious, Eric Holder, or what Obama's policies have done to the economy with the same fervor he went after conservatives?

Come to think of it, how often did you hear Jeb Bush opposing the Obama Regime? Former First Lady Barbara Bush was critical of the "harsh tone" of the 2012 GOP primary (see that as the vetting of Romney), but where was she while the American people were suffering under the harshness of the Obama Regime's statist policies?

I could probably write an entire book on how the Republican Party establishment goes after its own base more than it ever does the Democrats, and maybe someday I will, but by now you get the picture.

Several times during the 2012 campaign I had newspaper reporters from across the country contact me for my take on what Romney has to do to rally his base for the general election. I always told them they were asking the wrong question.

The question isn't whether or not Romney would be able to successfully rally his base—the question is whether or not he actually wants to.

His people demanded Republican National Committee members sign some ham-fisted "loyalty pledge" that smacks of a George Orwell plot device. His people tried to alter the party rules to stifle the increasing Tea Party/liberty influence. If this was Romney wanting to woo us, he had a funny way of showing it.

---

79 Debra Heine, "Jeb Bush to Award Hillary Clinton with 2013 Liberty Medal," Breitbart News, June 28, 2013, http://www.breitbart.com/InstaBlog/2013/06/28/Jeb-Bush-To-Award-Hillary-Clinton-With-2013-Liberty-Medal

Ladies, imagine for a second the guy you're interested in rarely if ever calls, takes no initiative to show you he cares, but then turns around and demands you give him the attention he desires whenever the mood suits him. After a while your girlfriends would urge you to salvage whatever shred of dignity you had left and admit that "he's just not that into you."

Let me share with you what I have learned fighting the Republican Party establishment through two presidential primary cycles, and what I shared with these reporters.

At best the Republican Party establishment views its grassroots base as (what kids today would refer to as) a hook-up or a booty call. At worst they outright hate us, because we're the reason GOP cronyists don't get away with pillaging and plundering the public trough for their buddies with the same reckless abandon as the Democrats.

The Romney campaign from day one had two prime directives: marginalize the influence of conservatives (especially Evangelicals) within the GOP, and then to defeat Obama. They wanted to prove so much they could win without us so they had an excuse to banish us to the kids' table after they do. That's why Romney never reached out to us, just as his predecessor McCain never did until putting Palin on the ticket, and then after her stunning speech at the Republican National Convention they never put her in a position to shine like that again.

See, in the GOP establishment's world, Palin is the reason McCain lost. Not the reason he actually didn't lose as bad as Walter Mondale or George McGovern did.

Losing is in these folks' DNA. They claim to be incrementalists, but they're really just defeatists. These folks would rather lose to Democrats than lose control of the Republican Party to us.

They just don't see it as losing, because losing to them isn't defined by not getting to govern. In fact, they would rather not have to govern so they can perpetually raise money off of the naive "sheeple" out there by proclaiming how bad the Democrats are all the time. Losing to them is defined as losing leverage, not elections. If they're not in charge, it's fine with them if the Democrats are.

The golden rule to them is "he who has the gold gets to make the rules." I'm not saying they don't care about the future of the country, it's just they define what's best for the future a lot differently than you or I do. They have more in common with Democrats than they do the patriots in the grass roots.

Mothers have been advising their daughters for eons that "he ain't gonna buy the cow if you give him the milk for free." Conservatives have been freely giving their "milk" to the Republican Party establishment for 30 years—and what do we have to show for it?

Is the government bigger or smaller? Are taxes and fees (a tax by another name) higher or lower? Is the country more or less secularized? Are government schools more or less likely to indoctrinate your kids with anti-American/anti-Christian propaganda? Our children, even our Christian children born and bred in the church, are poised to undo all of this nation's moral foundations in the name of wrongly defined tolerance.

We must come to grips with the fact the Party of Reagan isn't the party of Reagan. Reagan was the Republican Party's aberration. From Ford, to Reagan, to both Bushes, to Dole, to McCain, and to Romney—one of these things is not like the other.

And it's Reagan.

The Republican Party is the party of big government. It just believes that having the complete statist monstrosity the Left wants is icky. It doesn't want to end child killing. It wants to regulate it. It doesn't want to oppose the homosexual agenda. It wants to moderate it. It doesn't want to return power back to the states and to the people. It wants to channel it toward its vested interests instead.

All conservatives have been doing via the GOP for this past generation is slowing down into a steady jog the breakneck slouch toward Gomorrah the Left desires. While the Democrats prefer the pedal to the medal, the Republican Party establishment is happy just leaving it on cruise control. But make no mistake, we head in the wrong direction no matter who wins. The only debate is about the rate of speed.

As former Congressman J.C. Watts once told me, "They just manage the decay."

These people tolerate us at best, and despise us at worst. They define their leadership by our followership. To them leadership isn't about setting an example of boldness and courage in advancing our principles; it's about getting the people and constituencies you presume to be under your control to do what you want them to do. A mainstream media reporter once told me off the record, "These ruling class Republicans you speak of really do think they're entitled to your vote."

In other words, it's about power—plain and simple.

The more we assert ourselves and try to take control of the process, the whinier they get. The more blatant and desperate they get to keep control, too. Like when Congressman Eric Cantor openly urged Democrats to cross over into the Republican primary to save establishment RINO Richard Lugar in his 2012 senate primary. Or when "Ditch" McConnell plays dirtier with his primary challenger in Kentucky, Matt Bevin, than he does President Obama.

Remember the friend I wrote about in my introduction that beat a well-funded Democrat from a powerful family despite getting no help from the Republican Party establishment? Do you know how the Republican Party establishment reacted to his win? The Republicrat governor appointed the Democrat he defeated to a position in his administration!

But that's the Republican Party establishment: snatching defeat from the jaws of victory since 1976.

This brings me to the sixth commandment: never, ever abandon your base (unless they're morally wrong).

The Republican Party establishment always ends up fighting a two-front war between its own base and the Democrats. Meanwhile, the Democrats come across as a united front. While that's not always the case, it appears that way because the Republican Party establishment consistently violates this commandment.

An example from my own state's legislature illustrates my point.

The Democrat state senate leader in my state is a fearless, hard-left ideologue. The sort of leader you love when he's on your team, hate when he's not. I can't recall a single time he's backed down to the Republicans on anything in the last five years. He ruthlessly pushes his agenda and rules with an iron fist. If any somewhat moderate Democrats (hey, I live in the heartland, there might still be a few) get squishy, they get rolled. On the other hand, he protects the true believers with all his might. This sends a message: if you're on board with the ideological agenda we've got your back, if you're not we don't.

Wouldn't you love this guy to be a conservative?

Then there was the Republican speaker in my statehouse. He views himself as a consensus builder, not an ideologue—which really means he's middle management. He doesn't like to bring things up for a vote unless they'll pass and everyone in his majority is on the same page. His number one goal is not to advance the issues in the party platform, rather it is to maintain a "family atmosphere" and turn conservatives into "team players." He's not a general, he's a babysitter.

You know, like John Boehner.

After getting the majority, he backed down on allowing votes on protecting Second Amendment rights and Personhood in an effort to protect the squishiest in his own caucus, who didn't want grassroots conservatives to know where they truly stood on the issues in order to avoid being primaried. He put consensus ahead of convictions, and by doing so drove a wedge right through the middle of his own base.

His problem is the newly-elected conservatives of 2010 didn't go to my state capitol to play footsy with Democrats and hold a never-ending schedule of fundraisers. They went there to get things done and go home. So instead of falling in line with the rest of the group-think, they used procedural motions to force Second Amendment and pro-life votes over the leadership's wishes.

By standing for unity for unity's sake, and not unifying his caucus around the principles that make us Republicans in the first place, my Republican speaker ended up fanning the very flames of conservative insurrection he was trying to douse. In the spring of 2012 my state had a record number of primaries, and the Republicrats lost almost all of them. The Republican Party establishment tried to blame it on redistricting, but the Democrats faced redistricting, too, and didn't face this level of internal turmoil.

Why is that?

Because their leader was leading on their issues. Our leader was the blind leading the blind. The Democrat leadership in my state legislature united around holding the line for the child killers, moral depravity lobby, educrats, and statists. The Republican leadership in my state legislature united around how they could diffuse conservative zeal so as to not offend the child killers, moral depravity lobby, educrats, and statists. One approach leads to a united base. The other abandons your base and leads to a two-front war.

A similar scene played out nationally during the great, over-hyped government shutdown of 2013. Rather than hold the line on defunding Obamacare, a majority of Senate Republicans sided with Harry Reid and against Senators Ted Cruz, Mike Lee, and the American people. Rather than holding the line on defunding Obamacare, House Speaker John Boehner used Democrat votes to cave.

This is what happens when you don't stand united on principle, but are a movement run by shills, gutless cowards, and feckless bureaucrats. There is no other way to spin this. Obama completely routed Republican "leadership." He removed the manly parts of the Republican leadership and showed it to them on a national stage. He completely de-panted them.

Obama hasn't done much right during his presidency, which is why when the chips are down he knows he can always pick a fight with Republican "leadership." They have acted as his reliable slump-buster throughout his presidency, and this time they came through big time.

I loathe the GOP establishment with all my heart, but even I pitied them in this case. They think they're getting out of their consultants' doghouse, but what they're really doing is signing their own death certificates.

Begrudgingly, give the devil his due. These statist progressives really know how to play the game. Then again, it helps when you actually believe in your cause. Right now, the people running "our side" don't believe in ours.

The Republican Party establishment is struggling with the fact we in the grassroots are fighting back. They're used to the previous generation that just wanted to be patronized, validated with a pointless proclamation or a pro-life license plate, and then went home to play bingo or watch *Murder She Wrote*.

I recall a one-on-one meeting I had with a Republicrat leader early in my radio career when I was really ornery. No, really, I've actually mellowed out a little bit!

Anyway, we were sitting down for breakfast, and as I'm eating my omelet he proceeds to lecture me about how naïve I am about how the political process works, and that I'm asking for too much. It sounded like a spiel he had given dozens of times to well-meaning but utterly harmless Christian Conservatives who just don't know any better, and think "thou must be nicer than God no matter what while hell ruthlessly advances" is the 11th Commandment inadvertently left out of the Bible.

He was about to find out I'm not one of those do-gooders who wears socks with sandals, and gets up in the morning with a pair of khakis on.

I let him ramble on unchallenged just long enough for me to finish my omelet. Forgive me, but I live in Iowa, where farm fresh food must come first. After I finished the last morsel I looked at him and asked him if it was okay for me to respond to what he was saying.

"Sure," he said.

I looked right at him and calmly said, "I want to quote for you the immortal words of the great prophet Nick Nolte in the movie *48 Hours*. 'We ain't partners, we ain't brothers, and we ain't friends.' I'm not a team player, and I don't want to be. I don't want to hang out with you, I already have a family and my schedule is full. I get up in the morning and go work out (even if it doesn't look like it), then I go to work. I come home and play with my kids. After my kids go to bed, I play with my wife. Then the process repeats itself the next day. Don't give me your card. I'm not giving you mine. I don't want your cell phone number, and I'm not giving you mine. I don't want to sit next to your political hacks at the party fundraiser. What I do want is for you to do your damn job, and that job is fighting for us on the issues we care the most about. If you do that I will be the best friend you've ever had, but if you sell us out I will make you hate life for three hours a day on a 50,000-watt radio station. Are we clear?"

"Crystal," he replied.

That's how it's done. That is how the employer (us) recovers the leverage with our employees (them). By the way, given his actions afterwards it was obvious he didn't get the message, but he's out of politics now and I'm still here so he ended up getting it after all.

These people work for us. They're not a ruling class, and they're not matinee idols on the cover of *Tiger Beat*. We must never forget that, and more importantly we must never let *them* forget it, either. We don't thank them for giving us our time, or pose for pictures with them like we're groupies. Does your boss thank you for your time when he needs you to do your darn job? Does your boss pose for pictures with you and ask for your autograph? We need to stop feeding the animals, and start reigning them in.

More and more of you are getting the picture, which is why more and more of them are losing their jobs. In the 2012 Texas Republican primary, 10 incumbents were defeated in one night! God bless Texas!

This trend needs to not just continue, but be ramped up even further. The Republicrats can't help but betray their own base, because they're not one of us. It's like I said earlier in this book, show me your faith (principles) and I'll show you your works. You know a tree by its fruit. We fight because we're fighting for what we believe in. They obstruct because they're trying to stop what they don't.

Unfortunately, it's not just the Republican Party establishment that violates this commandment, but sometimes conservatives as well.

Take for example a man I really like. Rick Santorum's social conservative street cred is above reproach. For years Santorum carried the water for social conservative causes and issues, earning the scorn of all the right people like the liberal media and Republicrats like John McCain.

Throughout the course of his underdog yet successful 2012 presidential campaign, he was the one candidate who most consistently defended America's Judeo-Christian moral tradition, and effectively demonstrated the linkage between the growth of government and America's moral decline.

So why did it take so long for Santorum to finally become the champion of this large bloc of values-voters?

Because a few years prior Santorum abandoned his base by endorsing Arlen Specter—a RINO's RINO—over Pat Toomey in a hotly contested Pennsylvania senate primary. In his next election, Santorum lost by 18 points, which remains one of the worst losses by an incumbent senator in American political history. When you throw in the fact Santorum wasn't saddled by a personal scandal, there is only one explanation for the magnitude of Santorum's defeat. Some of his base stayed home believing it wasn't worth it to go to the polls for someone they felt had abandoned them.

Years later I saw this on the 2012 Iowa Caucus campaign trail. Santorum was a frequent guest on my program, and every time he came on I would receive several calls, emails, and Facebook posts from conservatives who wanted me to ask him about his Specter endorsement. That endorsement was seen as such a betrayal that many conservatives treated Santorum as if he didn't have a record in the U.S. Senate that on several key issues would've been one of the most conservative of his era. It was like Santorum had become his middle name, and he was now known as Rick Santorum "who endorsed Arlen Specter." I know a couple of Iowa Caucus activists that wouldn't agree to support Santorum until he looked them in the eye and promised he'd never endorse someone like Specter again.

By the way, Santorum said one of the reasons he made a bargain with Specter to help him in his primary was because Specter promised to help shepherd President George W. Bush's judicial appointments through the testy nomination process (Specter was chairman of the Senate judiciary committee at the time). One of those appointments Santorum wanted Specter's help with is now Chief Justice John Roberts, a man who did as much damage to the Constitution in one week in 2012 than most liberals can only hope to achieve in a lifetime.

Roberts was the deciding vote in the U.S. Supreme Court telling the sovereign state of Arizona it has no authority to enforce the U.S. Constitution, even though the sovereignty of the states precedes the Constitution, and the Constitution required ratification from the states to become law (government by the consent of the governed).

Then Roberts was the deciding vote in telling the federal government it has unlimited jurisdiction into the lives of American citizens, provided it uses the 16th Amendment as the means to tread on us. Roberts was even willing to allow the federal government to tax us for what we're not doing, which is unprecedented in American history. By positing this Roberts went so far as to re-structure the mandate within Obamacare as a spoonful of sugar to help the medicine go down. If that's not legislating from the bench, I don't know what is.

These two opinions by Roberts are not just unconstitutional—they are *anti-constitutional*. They clearly are anti both the spirit and explicit wording of the U.S. Constitution, which is intended to limit the jurisdiction of the federal government in order to maximize the freedom and liberty of the individual (as well as that of *these* United States of America).

Fast forward to 2012 and Toomey returned the favor by endorsing Romney over Santorum in the Pennsylvania presidential primary. Much of the Republican infrastructure in that primary, still smarting from Santorum's Specter endorsement, also opposed Santorum and supported Romney. Faced with the prospect of a potential loss in his home state primary, Santorum dropped out rather than risk an embarrassing defeat that at-worst would have ended his political career, and at-least would have undone a lot of the good he accomplished in his campaign up until that point.

A good Catholic like Santorum will understand what I mean

when I say Faustian Bargains never pay off. Santorum is not alone in needing to learn that lesson.

As of the time this book was being written, Kentucky Senator Rand Paul was poised to inherit not just his father's revolution, but also expand it into the ranks of social conservatives who like him but were skeptical of his father's Libertarian bent. However, Paul angered some of his father's long-time supporters when he endorsed Romney for president after his father suspended his bid. His father never did endorse Romney.

And it wasn't just that he endorsed Romney, it was the way he did it. He heaped more praise on Romney on Fox News than liberal Republican Rudy Giuliani did. He even started repeating the same old talking points about having to work within the system. Hardly the talk of revolution.

Except people didn't join his father's revolution to work within the system. Revolutions want to topple systems. They joined his father's movement to drain thc swamp. Paulistas correctly see the system as unsalvageable. They were hoping Rand would inherit his father's revolution, but smooth out his father's rough edges when it comes to presentation. This is not what they had in mind.

One of the things Rand said in his defense at the time is the exact same flawed thinking that led the Religious Right down the primrose path for the past 30 years, as my last book *We Won't Get Fooled Again: Where the Christian Right Went Wrong and How to Make America Right Again* portrays in vivid detail. Rand said that he was close to getting a vote on auditing the Federal Reserve, something his father has advocated for years, and that the leadership of the Republican Party would be more willing to give him the vote that was important to him if he supported the party's presidential nominee, unlike his father.

That is flat-out wrong. In fact, the exact opposite is true.

The only reason the Republican Party would be willing to provide Rand Paul a vote on auditing the Fed is because they're scared to death at what his father was able to accomplish in spite of them the past few years. In 2008 Ron Paul was getting laughed off the national stage as a quack for campaigning for president on auditing the Fed. Four years later, almost all of his 2012 GOP campaign rivals had at least tacitly signed on to the concept.

Why?

Well, I suppose it's because they had all sincerely seen the light, but like it says in my favorite country song, "Don't pee on me and tell me it's raining."

More likely it's because Ron Paul nearly won the 2011 Iowa Straw Poll, then nearly won the 2012 Iowa Caucuses, then got 40% of the vote one-on-one against Romney in the 2012 Virginia primary, and then saw his people take over the Republican Party in states like Maine, Nevada, Minnesota, and Iowa. The system is scared to death of the Ron Paul Revolution, so they're trying to patronize it by offering a symbolic vote—which will fall a few votes short of winning, of course—in the hopes it will be satisfied by this contrivance the way Christian Conservatives were satisfied with such milquetoast for 30 years beforehand.

Always remember my fellow patriots who are challenging the system: whenever the system offers you something, you already have it; and that's actually the entry point where the real negotiating starts. Except you shouldn't negotiate at all, but accept nothing less than unconditional surrender when the future is at stake for our children and grandchildren.

Look to Alexander the Great for inspiration.

In 331 B.C. King Darius was attempting to stop upstart Alexander the Great's quest to conquer his empire. He sent Alexander a letter promising him a substantial portion of his territory and his daughter's hand in marriage if Alexander would agree to stand down. Alexander responded, "What you offer me is already mine. As for your daughter, if I want to marry her, I will."

In 330 B.C. Alexander the Great conquered Darius' empire.

If Rand Paul wants a real vote on auditing the Fed, then he should leverage the base he inherited from his father to force that vote upon the system by threatening them with it. That's how real reform happens, not by settling for scraps from the establishment's table.

By playing the game instead of forcing the establishment's hand, all over the internet Paulistas were turning on Rand, and then turning on each for doing so. For example, one of the most active Ron Paul loyalists on Facebook posted this as his status update after Rand's endorsement of Romney, paraphrasing some of Rand's justification: "I don't understand why people are upset about Rand Paul endorsing Mitt Romney. Sometimes when you fight for principles, you have to make compromises in order to ensure personal gain. Remember what Winston Churchill said during the Battle of Britain: 'England was always my first choice, but hey; Germany looks stronger right now so it is time to join them. Hitler, he comes from a large family, so we have that connection.'"

Ouch—that's gonna leave a mark.

Now, in Rand's defense he got it right a few months later when he filibustered the U.S. Senate over the disclosure President Obama had a secret drone kill list intended to target American citizens. "Stand with Rand" became not just a meme that night but a movement. Several of Rand's contemporaries, like Texas Senator Ted Cruz, came alongside him during that filibuster. That's the kind of leadership people are looking for. They're looking for champions who take on the system, not cater to it.

Catering to the system is just what the hackneyed GOP establishment wants. Divide and conquer is the oldest strategy of them all. The Republican Party establishment is a Zen master when it comes to pitting conservative "leaders" against actual conservatives. We send leaders to Washington or our state capitols to fight on our behalf. Eventually they wear them down little by little until they become fully institutionalized by the system, and finally they return home to fight *us* for the system instead of fighting the *system* for us.

By turning our leaders into their human shields, the Republican Party establishment deflects scrutiny and pressure from us to perform where it matters most—public policy. I used to think the GOP stupidly fell into this trap of perpetual civil warfare out of cowardice, but eventually I figured out this was their plan all along. They co-opt our leaders so we believe we're fighting them, when we're really fighting each other.

That's why one of the last, best hopes we have for reform via political activism in this country is the Tea Party Movement, because it's spontaneous combustion. The longer the Tea Party movement avoids the temptation of creating a cabal of high-profile leaders perpetually on the Sunday morning talk shows and pretending to speak for the people, the better its chances to accomplish some real good. When the system pressures the Tea Party to become more organized, what it really means is "hurry up and appoint some ambitious spokespeople so we know specifically who we have to buy off and co-opt."

In an interview I did once with David Barton of Wallbuilders, he put it this way:

> I think we've hurt our integrity, but I think that is now a thing of the past. A lot of that was a reflection of the fact that we came through a paradigm where we were very top centered in our organizations. In other words, you had the Moral Majorities, and you had these other groups, and you had a spokesman for them and everybody marched to that tune. That is really fragmented now. You no longer have a national spokesman to do these things. You now have a thousand local groups that are doing these things. I think that has returned some credibility in the sense that they're just not shills. You have to deal with local leaders now and you have to deal with local groups. You have to deal with things at different levels.
>
> Who's the leader of the Tea Party groups? They don't have a leader. Nobody has a clue, and I think that's a healthy thing because that's virally driven, grassroots working up. We just had an incident here in Texas where for the first time in my lifetime we had 142 groups come together on a political issue telling the Speaker of the House, you've got the wrong committee chairman. I've never seen 142 groups come together on anything, but that's because they're all now philosophically united and they come from all spectrums— some are economic groups, some are social groups, but they all have a united vision.

Whenever you hear the following phrases from your "leaders," know that you in the conservative base are about to be abandoned or already have been:

- "You have to be more realistic."
- "That's not how we do things around here."
- "That's the way we've always done things."
- "Rome wasn't built in a day."
- "We'll get 'em next time/session."
- "Half a loaf is better than none."
- "We either hang together, or we'll hang alone." (Which is a total bastardization of this famous line from Benjamin Franklin, who was talking about everyone risking it all for liberty, when the system is talking about individuals risking nothing for re-election.)
- "You have to work within the system."

When your leaders start regurgitating these Republicrat clichés back to you in the grassroots, get them out of the system and back home as soon as possible to get them around some good influences before it's too late. Remember, bad company always corrupts good character.

Earlier in this book we cited the four pillars of the Left's power base—the child killing industry, the homosexual agenda, educrats, and government sector employee unions. When was the last time you saw Democrat national leadership or prominent Democrats anywhere in the country abandon any of these bases? The Left goes to war for their base, even to the point of shutting down the government or losing an election. Like when Vice President Joe Biden said the Left would shut the government down if Republicans on Capitol Hill insisted on de-funding Planned Parenthood during the debt ceiling showdown of 2011, or when President Obama came out against marriage the day after North Carolinians affirmed it by almost 30-points. Forty percent of Democrats in North Carolina voted to affirm marriage as well, but they weren't the Democrats that represent the four pillars the Left never abandons. Most of them were white working class and black Democrat voters.

We have seen the Left abandon ethnic and racial minorities, as well as private sector unions, but we never see them abandon and betray the child killing industry, the homosexual agenda, educrats, and government sector employee unions. So if you're a racial and ethnic minority, single mom, or a working class white that is a member of a private sector union, you need to know where you stand with the Democrats. It's quite simple, really—you don't. Or at the very least you stand in the back of the line behind Planned Parenthood, LGBT (or is it now LGBTQABCDEFG—do these people ever stop adding letters?), NEA, and AFSCME. You're their booty call. They use you when it's an election, but have no use for you after that.

Now let's look at the three groups that make up the traditional Reagan Coalition: values voters (pro-life/pro-family voters), limited government advocates (tax reformers/pro-growthers, Libertarians, etc.), and those who believe in a strong national defense (peace through strength). The Republicans have traditionally been seen as the strong national defense party, but there is little doubt and lots of evidence they have abandoned those of us in the other two groups repeatedly.

In politics you are what hills you're willing to die on. So based on their actual records of the past two decades, and not the rhetoric, we would say the leadership of the Democrat Party is for child killers, moral depravity, Islamists, anti-American progressive intellectuals, and statists. On the other hand, we'd have to say the leadership of the Republican Party is for morally indifferent crony capitalists that think it's our job to be the world's rent-a-cop.

I'm guessing that's not the Republican Party most of you reading this signed up for. At this point the Republicrats are beyond salvaging, and just need to be repealed and replaced, to borrow a phrase popular these days. But when we replace them with our own people, they must not make the mistake of abandoning us for them.

And if they do, we treat traitors accordingly.

8

Define Your Opponent Before They Define Themselves, and Define Yourself Before Your Opponent Defines You

There's this girl you're really interested in, and you really want to meet her, but you're too nervous to go up and introduce yourself.

So you ask your worst enemy to do it for you, who's attracted to her as well.

He proceeds to tell her about this guy he knows that's interested in her, piquing her curiosity. "Tell me about him," she says. "Is he cute?"

"Define cute," he replies. "I wouldn't say he's hideous, but he's certainly nothing special."

Granted, you're not exactly Ryan Reynolds or George Clooney, but you didn't have a problem getting a date in high school.

"Is he athletic or normal size," she asks (translation: is he morbidly obese).

Sure, now that you're a little older you're not as lean and mean as you once were, but you're still in pretty decent shape for your age.

"Dude could stand to lose a few pounds," is how your enemy describes you to her.

Now the girl is grasping for any initial reason to pursue this further. "What does he do for a living," is her final inquisitive attempt to give you a chance.

You're just about finished with med school, which you put off for a few years to do missionary work in Africa. Currently you volunteer to provide medical care at the homeless shelter in your spare time, and you're temporarily living at home with your mother, who is still lonely and struggling with grief after the unexpected death of your father last year.

Nevertheless, your enemy tells the girl "he's unemployed and lives at home with his mom."

By allowing your enemy to define you to the girl you're both interested in, you have been defined as unemployed and living at home with mom, overweight, and not exactly blessed with movie star looks. Your enemy didn't technically lie in the way he described you to the girl, but he certainly cast you in the worst possible light. Since the girl assumes she's already getting the best possible description of who you are from the person you sent to indirectly represent you, she concludes you're really a fat loser without a job.

"No wonder he didn't come talk to me himself," she says to her friends after your enemy departs—with her phone number for himself.

If you went online looking for love would you put "fat loser without a job" on your E-Harmony profile? No, you'd probably put "decent looking guy finishing up med school who is currently caring for his grieving mother" instead.

By now some of you reading this are wondering what the point here is, other than the shy guy who sent his enemy to talk to the girl he's interested in is a total ignoramus?

That's precisely the point.

In the culture war we are making the exact same mistake. We're bashful about expressing and advancing our principles, which allows our enemies to bash us to an available and undecided culture. Most Americans do not know what they really believe let alone why they believe it. Think I'm wrong? Just look at the election results of the past 12 years.

In 2000 the American people gave George W. Bush the presidency despite losing the popular vote. In 2002 the American people gave the Republicans both houses of Congress to go along with the presidency for the first time since Herbert Hoover. In 2004 they re-elected George W. Bush President of the United States. Then in 2006 they made Nancy Pelosi the first female Speaker of the House in American history, and gave the Democrats a 60-seat, filibuster-proof majority in the U.S. Senate. In 2008 they elected Barack Obama to the presidency and gave Democrats total control of Congress. In 2010 they fired over 700 Democrats and made Republican John Boehner Speaker of the House, sending a message to Obama he had gone too far left too fast. Then right after repudiating Obama in 2010, they turned right around and re-elected him in 2012 despite the fact he continued to govern just as he had prior to his 2010 midterm defeat.

Those are some dramatic swings in momentum in a relatively short amount of time. If I were analyzing the mood of the American electorate based strictly off those schizophrenic results, I'd have to conclude the American people want a quasi-socialist welfare state they don't want to have to pay for, a strong national defense they don't want to have to actually use, and a return to traditional morals they themselves don't want to be held accountable to.

Ours is a nation up for grabs, where marriage wins 32 consecutive elections all over the country, but most people no longer view homosexual behavior itself as immoral and can't get enough of *Modern Family*. Most Americans describe themselves as Christians, but then sit idly by and do nothing while every vestige of Christianity is snuffed out of our public institutions. Most Americans want less government until it's their suckling spot on the welfare state teat being threatened. We've gone from red states and blue states to red counties and blue counties, and now to red suburbs and blue inner cities in the same counties. One local weather forecaster says today will be partly sunny, and the guy on the other channel says it will be mostly cloudy.

We are every bit a house divided.

About the only thing we can agree on is we're desperate for leadership, and desperation almost always leads to bad decisions. Just like the stereotypical single woman in her 30s who lowers her dating standards due to her proverbial ticking biological clock, there is a palpable sense in the country the clock is ticking on America so "something must be done." I believe that sense of desperation, more than anything, is why we've seen such a schizophrenic voting pattern in the 21st century. We're basically trying anything to see what works, which is the political equivalent to grasping at straws or casting lots. We're one step away from just determining public policy via Powerball.

Aside from the hard left that wants to turn America into a Western European-style socialist democracy, most Americans are unsure of what they want. But after looking at what the leadership in both parties serves up after we empower them (meet the new boss, same as the old boss), we know what it is we don't.

In 2009 a friend of mine gave me some internal polling done for inside-the-beltway Republicans about the mood of the American electorate heading into the 2010 mid-terms. If I could sum up this report in one sentence it would be this: the American people don't like the Democrats and don't trust the Republicans. I think the same largely remains true today.

It used to be younger generations who had yet to face the real world were too idealistic, but now the exact opposite is true. The younger you go in America the more cynical you get, as generations that have never been taught the traditional American view of law and government—let alone history—become increasingly nihilistic. Just look at the video games they play, where the car thief and the assassin are the heroes. Altruism and absolutes are considered archaic. For 50 years Superman was America's comic book secular messiah. Nowadays the concept of someone doing good just because it is objectively good, and not being conflicted about whether it's actually good or not, just doesn't resonate with this generation. So Batman the damaged vigilante, who tight-ropes the razor's edge between light and dark, is the alpha super male instead.

Maybe it's just me, but I see this as a tremendous opportunity for us.

A theologian by the name of D. A. Carson observes that truth in a culture tends to work in a three-generation cycle: what one generation believes, the next generation assumes, and the third generation rejects. Obviously the truth that Carson is specifically referring to in his philosophical study is the Gospel, but since the Gospel played such an integral part in the making of America in the first place, it could be argued his analysis applies to our current cultural condition as well.

The greatest generation was the last one to embrace the foundational framework of the American way (e.g. personal responsibility, rugged individualism, American exceptionalism, etc.). The next generation, the baby-boomers, immediately began to splinter. Some formed what David Horowitz describes as the "New Left," thus sparking the so-called culture war. The majority of that generation, Republican and Democrat, assumed the beliefs of their parents in the greatest generation—but it only takes one bad apple to ruin the whole bunch.

With most of the baby-boom generation on cruise control, the New Left takes over the leadership of the Democrat Party and also takes control of most of the media, pop culture, and education infrastructure in the country. Now the third generation, adults my age and younger, have all but rejected what their grandparents believed to be true.

While that means we're culturally holding on for dear life here in the short run, if we can hold on long enough and play our cards right the long-term future has the potential for a major American Renaissance/Revival. The emerging generation is poised to begin the three-generation cycle all over again, the only question is what meta-theme or transcendent truth(s) will they embrace and pass on from there.

We've got a shot to restore the republic, but we've only got one shot.

In light of that, I've got some good news and some bad news. The good news is that emerging generation is all but a blank slate, believing in nothing. The bad news is we're not currently equipped to fill in the blanks for them.

We're now the counter-culture and the Left is now "the man keeping them down." It's becoming passé to have sex with anything you want short of a car battery, get stoned every day that ends in "y," and know nothing. That used to be cool, and considered some existential statement about refusing to be a cog in the machine, but now it's a cliché. Even raunchy comedy movies like *Knocked Up* have an underlying theme paying homage to some vestige of the Judeo-Christian moral ethic. If you want to challenge the status quo in this era you get and keep a job, pay your own way, stay married to the same person from the opposite gender until one or both of you die, have a lot of kids, and go to church.

In other words, the 1950s is now considered edgy.

The more hopeless it becomes, the more conditions on the ground in this culture are ripe for revival. Human nature craves complacency. As someone that has lost almost 100 pounds, I can personally vouch for this. I could talk all I wanted to about getting healthy, but only when I was sick and tired of being sick and tired did I truly commit to the change that was necessary. Otherwise, if we can kick the can down the road we will.

Along those lines, when faced with national fiscal insolvency, a generation's basic survival instinct takes over. This explains why Ron Paul—an almost octogenarian whose quirky stage presence makes Ross Perot look like Cary Grant—was one of the only Republicans in America successfully wooing young voters when he retired in 2012, despite the fact several of his domestic policy proposals are perhaps the most radically right-wing in the GOP.

Those younger voters are looking at a bleak future, and are rejecting the premise they have an obligation to accept the burden of the previous generation's inability or unwillingness to practice self-control or govern itself. On the other hand, elderly voters who belong to AARP no longer buy green bananas, let alone worry about what shape the country is in 20 years from now. They're voting based on maximizing their welfare state cash value now.

However, we will not be able to reach this emerging generation and position this country for a long-term rebound without obeying the seventh of my 10 Commandments of Political Warfare: define your opponent before they define themselves and define yourself before your opponent defines you.

Almost all of the terminology we take for granted our culture has redefined to the point the emerging generations are ignorant of what we're talking about. They have become living, breathing examples of the Hegelian Dialectic, which is when the thesis (the argument) and its antithesis (counter-argument) end up merging into a synthesis (narrative), and they become virtually indistinguishable from one another.

I see this when dealing with the liberal media, whom I've had a lot of interaction with the past couple of years as someone interviewed on presidential politics frequently. Older liberal reporters are Watergate-era ideologues naturally suspicious of conservatives and Republicans. However, when I've dealt with younger members of the liberal media I see a completely different level of bias. While their elders have rejected what conservatives believe, the next generation is totally ignorant of it.

They have been so indoctrinated into a secular progressive worldview that the idea of someone like me who can articulate a cogent thought, and still believe Jesus Christ physically rose from the dead, just doesn't compute. I am a foreign concept to them. They talk to me inquisitively, almost like they're saying "wow, these things do exist and we get to observe one of them in its natural habitat."

Let me provide three examples.

Older liberal media used the term "pro-choice" to describe those in favor of child killing. Younger liberal media now uses the term "reproductive freedom."

Older liberal media used the terms "gay marriage" or "same-sex marriage" to describe two people of the same gender committing to a monogamous relationship recognized by the state with the same prominence as marriage. Younger liberal media now uses the term "marriage equality."

Older liberal media used phrases like "making the wealthy pay their fair share" to play class warfare. Younger liberal media now goes straight-up socialist with the term "income equality."

Younger liberal media use phrases that leave no room for discussion, let alone debate. They are operating under the assumption that these questions have been settled, so considering other points of view is unnecessary since there aren't any that are valid. I've had many of them flat-out tell me I forfeit my right to free speech and religious liberty if I disagree with redefining marriage since I'm a "bigot," and bigots don't have rights. This, of course, is extremist language coming from those who call us extremists.

Since conservatives have spent a generation retreating from the arena of ideas to form holy huddles in our own little enclaves of the already-initiated, we have forsaken an entire generation to be indoctrinated by anti-American/anti-Christian Leftists who clearly know what they're doing.

The emerging generation hasn't rejected the American way. It hasn't even considered it.

We've stopped competing in the arena of ideas, so we've left them with no choice but to accept the synthesized narrative (Hegelian Dialectic) they've been sold in government school. Thus, they believe the Constitution calls for the separation of church and state, there is no such thing as transcendent truth, and moral absolutes don't exist. So if we're going to engage this emerging generation, we're going to have to define our terms and ourselves clearly and explicitly.

If there's one of our tactics that needs a complete overhaul, it's this one. We're still speaking Beta-Max/VHS, and the culture (especially the emerging generation) is speaking Blue-Ray. One of the best books on this subject I have ever read is *Beyond Belief to Conviction* by Josh McDowell.

McDowell talks about how terms that used to have a consensus definition in past generations now mean totally different things. The best example is the term "tolerance."

Tolerance used to mean, "I may not agree with what you're doing or what you believe, but as long as you're not doing anything illegal and your business stays your business, then it's no business of mine."

Now tolerance means, "You must accept, validate, and then participate in everything I am doing that is not illegal, and not only must it be your business but your children's business as well."

That's just one example of how we have lost the language here. In this media-driven age of mass communication and social networking, he who controls the language has control. Even our attempts to combat this have been ineffective. For instance, in a misguided attempt to appear culturally relevant and sensitive, the past generation of conservative leaders created their own code words like "traditional values" to avoid saying "Judeo-Christian" or "Biblical." In other words, they redefined their terms to appease their enemies.

Ironically, these code words are actually more offensive than the real words. When I tell someone who disagrees with me I am taking this stand because I am a Christian, they may not agree but since they're usually not a Christian they at least understand that disagreement is coming from my bitter clinging to my guns and my religion.

However, if I tell them I am taking this stand because I'm for "traditional values," I just told them they have no values, or that their values are out of the mainstream when the mainstream is currently preaching their values. Therefore, my attempt to soften the blow just created more enmity instead. Good luck finding common ground or bringing them over to your side from there.

What I have found when interacting with those who don't share my worldview is the exact opposite is true. The more I clearly define what I believe and why I believe it, the more credibility I develop with them, and the more willing they are to engage me in the arena of ideas—provided I do one thing.

I must apply my standard consistently.

Translation: the Bible and the Constitution must be equally applied to Democrats *and* Republicans.

Since we are no longer a silent majority in this country, we cannot just continue to subjectively admonish Democrats and provide Republicans political exoneration for their violations of the "Laws of Nature and Nature's God" and expect to get our way on Election Day. In this next phase of the culture war, we're going to need converts to our side, and in this day and age no one wants to sign up with a bunch of hypocrites. If we want the culture at-large to accept our truth claims then we must have integrity in applying them.

I define integrity as a consistency between right belief and right behavior, or long obedience in the right direction. Without integrity there is no trust. Without trust there is no relationship. Without relationship there is no hope of getting others to see things your way. As the old saying goes, "No one cares what you know until they know how much you care."

The American people don't believe we really believe these principles like limited government and Judeo-Christian morality we're clamoring for all the time, because they see our unwillingness to hold Republicans to the same standard as Democrats. They think all we care about is beating Democrats, and not what's best for the country. Sadly, too many conservative groups have fed this stereotype. We have been defined as hypocrites, and every time we do something like spend three years scourging the evils of Obamacare, only to turn right around and anoint the architect of its predecessor Romneycare our presidential nominee, we end up playing right along with their narrative.

Another recent hypocrisy perfectly illustrates my point. In 2012 the Republican Chairman of the Armed Services Committee said allowing homosexuals to openly serve in the U.S. military was a "settled" issue, and Republicans would not seek to repeal it. This after years of Republicans fighting the repeal of "don't ask don't tell," which is one of the few culture war issues John McCain has actually been willing to stand for.

But now a Republican majority in the U.S. Congress won't seek to reassert the policy it fought against being repealed, and hammered Democrats for? Then what was the point in the first place? Not to mention, if a Democrat Chairman of the Armed Services Committee had said that every pro-family group in the country would've flooded my email inbox with fundraising calls to "fight the liberals trying to impose their Hollywood values on the rest of us."

We may view ourselves as conservatives, constitutionalists, and/ or Christians, but the reality is we have allowed our enemy to define us as hypocrites, which is our own fault. Attacks are only damaging when they're true. Someone can accuse me of beating my wife all they want, but as long as she comes out and says it's not true it says more about them than it does me. Therefore, the damages that come from being attacked are always self-inflicted, either because you are who they say you are, or you failed to respond accordingly or with a tin ear. All other attacks are opportunities, with your attackers providing you with the means, motive, and opportunity to define yourself without sounding like you're self-righteous or a self-promoter.

We are also allowing our enemies to define the argument.

Why do pro-life groups just accept being labeled "anti-abor tion?" Why do pro-family groups accept being labeled "anti-same sex marriage?" When did illegal aliens become "undocumented immigrants?"

How come conservatives allow these characterizations to go unchallenged when they're being interviewed or communicating via their own platforms? Why do conservatives accept Orwellian, politically-correct double-speak like "pro-choice" or "sexual orientation," and then expect to actually win the argument after the other side has already framed it?

After all, the right to life is the default position of the Declaration of Independence, which is the organic law of the United States. So shouldn't those who oppose that right be described as "anti-life" or "pro-death?"

Marriage as the union between one man and one woman is among the oldest traditions in the 5,000 years of recorded human history, so shouldn't those who seek to undo it be described as "anti-marriage?"

One of the reasons conservatives get a bad rap for only being defined by what they're against is because, well, we allow ourselves to be defined by what we're against.

We must stop allowing the Left to define us and the argument if we actually want to win the argument. A pretty good rule of thumb is if this is how your enemy wants to be defined, or wants to define you, you don't want to use that definition.

For example, two terms we should never use—that's right, *never* use—are abortion and sexual orientation.

Abortion sounds indifferent to what is actually taking place, which is intentional. When your kid is getting his tonsils out, the doctor calls it a tonsillectomy. So how come when a mother is having her child removed it's not called a pediaectomy? Probably because there'd be a lot less of them if it had been defined all along by what it is—child killing.

Whenever pro-lifers are using a public platform to defend the God-given, unalienable right to life, we need to define child killing as child killing. Would you rather be pro-choice or pro-child killing?

Some of you reading this will balk immediately at what I just wrote worried such coarse language comes across as offensive. If you're one of those people, then start over at the beginning of this book and re-read. If after re-reading you still don't get it, then do the rest of us a favor and get out of politics because you're not cut out for it. Doesn't mean you're a bad person, it just means you're not cut out for warfare and only getting in the way of victory.

I guess I'm kind of strange, because I'm more worried about offending the God our politicians swear their oath of office to who hates the shedding of innocent blood, then I am offending the ones shedding that innocent blood. I guess I'm more worried about saving babies then I am upsetting those killing them. We would not consider calling a serial killer pro-choice for choosing to take the lives of innocent people, so why would we refer to those who have assented to the slaughter of at least 50,000,000 American citizens in such antiseptic terms?

It's quite simple, really. If you want to raise awareness among the American people in order to move them to stop child killing, then you should probably define it as child killing. It's no wonder abortion ranks low among the issue priorities for many Americans, because that sounds indifferent and impersonal. However, many of those same Americans—regardless of belief system—would instinctively act right away if someone was threatening innocent children in their neighborhood. Calling child killing what it is goes a long way towards creating a similar sense of urgency.

Likewise, there's no such thing as sexual orientation. This term implies the natural gender each of us is born with is somehow insufficient in determining our identity, when nothing could be further from the truth. To agree to that premise would require me to say God makes mistakes.

I don't put windshield wiper fluid in my gas tank and then expect the car to run properly because it has a different "fuel orientation." The intelligent designer of the car intended for the parts he designed to work together for a reason, and the car doesn't work properly unless we use it as its designer intended. Similarly, males and females created in the image of God each have parts the other doesn't have. Those parts fit together, and it just so happens the primary purpose they fit together is for procreation. Amazing, isn't it? Almost like there was a plan or something.

If we don't get a grip on the language here, the next stop will be the *Twilight Zone*. Here's what happens when a culture reaches the *Twilight Zone*. In an era defined by bad ideas whose time has come, this one ranks right up (or should I say down) there.

As of November 2013 parents in Germany will now be given a third option[80] for defining their child's gender on his/her birth certificate. No, I didn't just make that up. Yes, you read that right.

But there aren't three genders you say? There are only boys and girls you claim?

Well, that's because you're still living in the dark ages with the rest of history's losers, bitterly clinging to your guns and your

---

80 Fredericke Heine, "M, F, or Blank: 'Third Gender' Officially Underway in Germany," *Spiegel*, August 16, 2013, http://www.spiegel.de/international/germany/third-gender-option-to-become-available-on-german-birth-certificates-a-916940.html

Bibles. See, you're still holding on to those antiquated traditions of Western Civilization—the very moral value system that made liberty and prosperity possible. As a progressive bureaucrat in Oregon recently said, you need to be rehabilitated.[81]

Once rehabilitated, you will come to learn what all the progressives currently saving Western Civilization have come to learn (although we have no idea where or how they learned it)—that a child's gender could be "indeterminate" as the German government now asserts.

True, for eons now humankind of all races, ethnicities, and belief systems simply looked between a newborn baby's legs to determine what gender he/she was and then raised it accordingly. But that's so passé. Just because we've been doing it that way for 5,000 years doesn't mean we should keep on denying each randomly evolved primate's quest for self-actualization. After all, who are we to judge? How can I possibly impose my definition of penis, vagina, male, or female on another human being?

If there is no standard we're all ultimately accountable to, then there really is no standard at all and everyone does what he/she sees fit. This chaos is what progressives describe as "freedom."

Granted, Western Civilization has traditionally defined "freedom" to mean freedom from our sinful nature, to do what's right without government redefining right from wrong to suit its own statist desires, and then to profit off of doing so. Thus we can pass on a better way of life to our gender-specific offspring than we had.

But why hold on to cherished traditions that built the most successful human civilization this side of Eden, when we instead can trade it all in for a culture so "indeterminate" we don't even know what gender we are? If only we could also get the progressive statists to throw in $17 trillion in debt as well to sweeten the deal? Wow, who wouldn't make that trade in a heartbeat?

Can you shout "Allahu, Akbar?" I hope so, because it looks like you'll need to sooner rather than later!

---

81 "Oregon to 'Rehabilitate' Businesses Opposed to Gay Marriage," *Red State,* August 20, 2013, http://www.redstate.com/2013/08/20/oregon-to-rehabilitate-businesses-opposed -to-gay-marriage/

Maybe you don't think this is your problem. Maybe you think whatever doesn't impact your wallet is none of your concern. Except the very people peddling this dead sprint towards Gomorrah are the same people that steal from you in the name of compassion. So either way, you will be made to care.

But why stop at the child's birth? We shouldn't impose a gender on a child ever. What blessed diversity that would be. Imagine gender becoming like an Almond Joy candy bar commercial from back in the day.

"Sometimes you feel like a nut, sometimes you don't."

But let's not overreact with one of those dreaded "slippery slope" arguments. It's not like we'll have kids in schools determining what bathrooms to use based on what gender they feel they are on a given day or anything.

Oh, wait . . . they already are doing that as we speak in California.[82]

If you want to save marriage and stop your children from being indoctrinated into believing that which God says is wrong is suddenly right, then don't accept the terminology of those doing that which you oppose. Previous generations that built this country didn't refer to someone's sexual orientation, they referred to someone behaving immorally—and so should we. Previous generations that built this country didn't refer to gender identity, they referred to men and women—and so should we. Please note the previous generations that built this country didn't have the systemic moral problems we currently have, so we would be wise to follow in their footsteps.

Oh, and please stop using terms like same-sex marriage, gay marriage, or traditional marriage. There is only marriage. What's next, referring to couples shacking up as pre-marriage? Everyone already knows what a marriage is, so accepting the premise that it can be redefined or clarified by either side is allowing our enemies to define us. Since we hold the moral high ground, we should be defining them.

---

82 Tim Donnelly, "Transgender Restroom Law Humiliates the 98%," *WND*, August 15, 2013, http://www.wnd.com/2013/08/transgender-restroom-law-humiliates-the-98/

Branding is so important in our culture. You may prefer Pepsi, but when you go to a movie or out to eat your default is to ask for a Coke. Mindshare always equals marketshare. The power of the brand becomes embedded in the subconscious of our fellow Americans, and if that branding is done by the American Left we are doing ourselves irreparable harm in the long run by reinforcing it.

Instead of reinforcing the Left's branding, we need to introduce our own.

9

Always Make Your Opponent Defend their Record/Belief System

Your Republican champion is ready to take on a notoriously liberal member of the mainstream media, who is a Democrat talking-point regurgitator masquerading as an objective journalist.

His show might as well be called "The Graveyard," because so many conservatives have gone there to die in the past that grassroots patriots wonder why Republicans even agree to do it at all anymore. "Keith" is snotty, snarky, and worst of all, smart. Like wickedly smart. The kind of guy you wish was on your side.

He's also not known for exchanging pleasantries, and goes right for the throat with his very first question.

"Mr. Republican, you have been critical of Democrats calling for more policies to help the poor and downtrodden in our abundantly wealthy society, saying they are too expensive and taxpayers shouldn't be asked to shoulder such a burden," he says. "It's easy for those who are well off like you to focus first on their own needs, and not the needs of others, but I believe I am my brother's keeper. You claim to be a Christian, so isn't it the moral thing to care for the less fortunate? Surely, in a country as wealthy as ours there is no excuse for poverty. Instead of tax cuts for the rich, shouldn't we put others less fortunate first?"

As he closes his mini-monologue masquerading as a question, the liberal host squares his shoulders and he begins to subtly strut like a peacock. "Keith" is confident because this line of emotion-based drivel has driven so many other previous Republicans into the fetal position on his program.

"Interesting take, Keith, how much do you think is enough," Mr. Republican asks the liberal host.

"Certainly in a $6 trillion economy there's enough to ensure income equality is there not," he says.

"Well if you believe so strongly in that principle, why don't you start by living it out in your own life," Mr. Republican says matter-of-factly.

"What are you talking about," Keith responds. "I'm not the public official here you are, so since you're the one making public policy you're the one who has the burden of proof."

"Nice try Keith," Mr. Republican says. "I may be making public policy, but you're trying to shape it and influence it. Therefore, your opinion matters at least as much as mine, and you're required to be at least as accountable as me. Therefore, perhaps your audience would be interested in knowing that you made $10.6 million last year according to industry trade reports?"

Keith gets a sly grin on his face. "Steady, Mr. Republican. That is what I made. But you made over $120 million last year according to your publicly released tax records. I'm doing well, but I'm not even in the same ballpark."

Mr. Republican smiles back winsomely. "It's true, my family and I have been very blessed. This is why last year we gave over $15 million to charitable causes like Animal Rescue League, homeless shelters, orphanages, and several overseas missionaries along with what we give back to our church. The reason you didn't get a press release on that is because my faith tells me not to publicize my giving for personal gain, but to give to others in honor of how much God has given me. I'm only bringing it up now because you brought up my personal financial situation, making it fair game."

"So you're touting the fact you gave $15 million to charity, which is more than I make in a year? You still have over a $100 million left after that, which is 10 times what I made," Keith says.

"Actually, after Uncle Sam takes his cut off the top my family ended up giving almost 20% of our income away, and that doesn't count the personal investments we made in stocks and real estate with our income that helped stimulate the economy by creating more jobs to handle those capital investments. How much did you give to charity last year?"

Keith is now starting to get fidgety.

"Off the top of my head I don't know," he says warily.

"Well let me help you with that," Mr. Republican says winsomely. "Just kidding, I couldn't access your tax records without committing a felony or going to work for the NSA. And since you're not a Tea Partier, you don't have to worry about the IRS auditing you. But would you say you're at least as charitable as the last Democrat vice president of the United States?"

"Absolutely, Joe is a fine man who loves his neighbor as he loves himself," Keith says, his confidence suddenly returned.

"Then you're in some dubious company, because according to their publicly released tax records the Bidens gave an average of $369 per year to charity in the 10 years prior to him becoming vice president when he was serving in the U.S. Senate. That's about 0.3 percent of his income."

Keith is now getting visibly flustered. "Well, well, those were the lean years of the Bush recession and money was kind of tight."

Mr. Republican now moves in for the kill. "Well, to your point the vice president's giving did go up after becoming Obama's vice president—to a grand total of 1.4 percent of his income. When you consider over 80% of Biden's income was from the taxpayers, and 100% of my family's income came from our own labors—I forego my salary as an elected official—and our private income was used to create jobs and opportunities for others, why don't we ask your audience who cares more for their fellow man?"

Keith gives Mr. Republican a condescending golf clap. "Well played, sir well played. I'll give you this; you've got more chutzpah than most of the Republicans that come on this show. Fine, I'll grant the point that you and your family have been successful, responsible, and charitable. But then why not extend that responsibility and charity to others? Regardless of what you're doing in your personal life, which I applaud, your public policy positions are abhorrent."

"Do you think I have a responsibility to be my brother's keeper," Mr. Republican asks.

"You bet I do, we all do," Keith replies.

"Keith, where does that idea come from, do you know?"

"It's just common decency," Keith answers.

Out of the corner of his eye, Mr. Republican sees the off-camera producer indicating it's almost time to take a commercial break, so he knows it's now or never for the money shot. In an unassuming tone of voice he says, "Actually Keith, given the fact you're an avowed atheist, I'm not surprised you don't know where the expression really comes from. The first recorded usage of the phrase 'brother's keeper' in human history came from a man named Cain, who sarcastically asks God 'am I my brother's keeper' after God begins to question him about why he murdered his own brother. I've always found it ironic when liberals quote the first murderer Cain to defend their warped view of compassion, since Cain had none . . . "

. . . Now the music starts up indicating the show is about to go to commercial break and "Keith" tries to get the final word, but Mr. Republican won't be denied . . .

". . . But then again I shouldn't be surprised since liberals such as yourself don't understand true compassion, as evidenced by the fact you've supported state-sanctioned child murder for decades now." And with a million dollar smile Mr. Republican closes with, "Cain would be proud of you, Keith."

"We'll be right back with tonight's worst person in the world," Keith sheepishly says.

COMMANDMENT #8 | 169

To the best of my knowledge, the hypothetical you just read has never actually occurred in my lifetime, but if it did it would've been the best thing ever.

Just once—once—wouldn't it be awesome to see something like this actually happen?

As a talk show host, I face an almost daily temptation to fire off the verbal and intellectual equivalent to the Enola Gay and drop neutron bombs. However, we need to remember weapons of mass destruction create collateral damage and fallout, and sometimes that fallout reaches your house. I'm not saying there's never a time for mushroom clouds, but I am saying I have had to learn the hard way there's never a time to do it all the time.

Besides, why drop a weapon of mass destruction when skilled precision does the job even better? In the current theater of political warfare we need fewer B-1 bombers and more skilled Navy SEAL types.

For example, in the hypothetical you just read, notice how often Mr. Republican uses a question to set up his antagonist. In a relatively short exchange, Mr. Republican asks "Keith" eight questions. The questions are framed skillfully and used purposefully. They are somewhat open-ended and at times non-threatening (on the surface) invitations to dialogue, but structured in a way that it forces the other side to reveal their own belief system when answering.

We must add this arrow to our quiver, because without it we end up arguing their premise and playing defense all the time.

Revealing the true motive and worldview of your opponent by asking questions, as opposed to debating opposing declarative statements, has been a devastating tactic used throughout history and is often utilized in the Bible. Often referred to nowadays as the Socratic Method, the use of questions to stimulate critical thought and deconstruct your adversary was used several times in the New Testament by Christ Himself.

These examples are particularly relevant today, because during His earthly ministry Christ was facing a philosophical predicament similar to what many American patriots are faced with today. Jesus was implementing a paradigm that challenged the corrupt established order. On one side were pagan authorities who opposed everything he stood for, but they were willing to leave him alone provided he kept his beliefs private and didn't challenge their powerbase. This, of course, is impossible for if we start sectioning off our faith from certain segments of our life we're disobeying our Lord, who demands we live out the faith His grace has provided us in every part of our lives.

On the other side were those who viewed themselves as subjectively good because they didn't see themselves as subjectively bad as the pagans, and they didn't understand why Jesus challenged them so directly when clearly they were the lesser of two evils.

Sounds a little familiar, doesn't it?

American patriots today are faced with a Democrat Party whose leadership wants to either re-write the U.S. Constitution or shred it altogether. But we're also faced with a Republican Party leadership that is either too corrupt or cowardly to oppose them, and then when we challenge them to do the job we elected them to do they sanctimoniously ask us why we're holding them accountable when the Democrats are so much worse?

We know the Democrats are bad, that's why we voted for the Republican. But we didn't vote for the Republican to give us piecemeal the exact same thing the Democrat would give us in bulk. We voted Republican to oppose the Democrat altogether and do what is right.

Similarly, God knew the religious and moral ethic of the pagan world was bad. That's why He established Israel to be a light to all nations. However, by the time Christ arrives on earth, the religious and moral authority in Israel had deviated so far from the original plan that early in Christ's earthly ministry he gives a message clarifying over a thousand years of religious teaching and tradition gone awry (the famous Sermon on the Mount). From that point forward it is clear to that wayward leadership Christ represents a threat, so they seek to first discredit Him and when that doesn't work to kill him instead.

They try to discredit him with gotcha questions devised to entrap Christ into saying something that would either cause the people rallying to Him to abandon Him, or draw the ire of the Roman authorities. Several times Jesus returns fire with a provocative question devised to reveal their true motives. Perhaps the two best examples of this would be:

> *Then the Pharisees went out and laid plans to trap him in his words. They sent their disciples to him along with the Herodians. "Teacher," they said, "we know you are a man of integrity and that you teach the way of God in accordance with the truth. You aren't swayed by men, because you pay no attention to who they are. Tell us then, what is your opinion? Is it right to pay taxes to Caesar or not?" But Jesus, knowing their evil intent, said, "Why are you trying to trap me? Show me the coin used for paying the tax." They brought him a denarius, and he asked them, "Whose portrait is this? And whose inscription?" "Caesar's," they replied. Then he said to them, "Give to Caesar what is Caesar's and to God what is God's." When they heard this they were amazed. So they left him and went away.*
>
> *While the Pharisees were gathered together, Jesus asked them, "What do you think about the Christ? Whose son is he?" "The Son of David," they replied. He said to them, "How is it then that David, speaking by the Spirit, calls him 'Lord'? For he says, 'the Lords says to my Lord: sit at my right hand until I put your enemies under your feet.' If then David calls him 'Lord,' how can he be his son?" No one could say a word in reply, and from that day on no one dared to ask him any more questions.*

When their attempts to discredit him failed, the sellout leaders now turn to the literal kill shot.

"Better for (Christ) to die than for all of us to perish," a compromised religious leader named Caiaphas says, foreshadowing the sort of sinister pragmatism we see from all too many contemporary Republicrats, who would rather lose to Democrats than lose control of the GOP to conservatives. Caiaphas is concerned that by Christ challenging the status quo, Christ will expose both he and his peers' hypocrisy while at the same time upsetting the

Roman authorities, prompting a violent backlash. In other words, Caiaphas fears man and not God.

Just like the Republicrats today who fear the backlash of the liberal media lynch mob more than they fear the God they swore their oaths of office to.

If you're a Christian, you know that Christ died for the sins of all humankind, so that through His sacrifice and resurrection we can be reconciled by grace through faith with our Creator. Therefore, Caiaphas didn't kill Christ anymore than the Romans did. We killed Christ every time we disobeyed God. But Caiaphas and the Romans didn't understand that and didn't see the bigger picture. They were operating under the very same myopic and amoral modus operandi the ruling class in our country utilizes today. It's about protecting one's turf, not about doing what's right. Contrast that with Utah Senator Mike Lee responding to snarky political commentators who asked him if the 2013 government shutdown was worth it: "It's always worth it to do the right thing."

Many of you reading this book already know this, which is why you're reading this book. That's why I didn't write this book to persuade you to follow the vision of our Founding Fathers. I wrote this book to help those of you who already are reach those among us who are not. Very few Americans are fully vested in a leftist, secular-progressive worldview. In fact, most Americans aren't fully vested in anything, and the Left takes advantage of that with its shallow talking points meant to tickle the ears of the masses they dumbed down in the government schools they control.

Therefore, if we're going to swell our ranks with the patriots it will take to restore our republic, we have to reach the uninitiated. Most of those people won't want to believe the bureaucrats and institutions they put their trust in all these years have sold out the country. Yes, they are informed enough to instinctively know something is wrong and don't like where the country is headed, but it's tough to go from complacency to conviction in one step.

This is why you hear people say stuff life, "I know Congress is corrupt but my congressman is a good guy." Or, "I can't believe some of the stuff they're teaching in the public schools nowadays. I sure am glad that doesn't happen at my kid's school."

Congress might be less popular than cockroaches and root canals, but 90% of Congressional incumbents were re-elected in 2012.

Becoming a parent has taught me a lot about discipleship. At first I thought I was discipling my kids, but I now know that God has also been using them to disciple me. One of the things you learn with kids is patience, and how to reward baby steps. Your kids just don't automatically get it. They are, as Rush Limbaugh would say, "young skulls full of mush." It is a step-by-step, nev-erending process. As a parent I have had to learn to consistently reward good behavior, and consistently punish bad behavior.

Too often parents become what Jen in my radio program's Amen Corner calls a "Walmart mom." Jen defines this as the mom at Walmart whose kids are acting up, so rather than doing the incon-venient thing by disciplining them in public, mom just buys them a treat or a trinket to shut them up. What "Walmart Mom" has now taught her children is that "the squeaky wheel gets the grease" when she should've taught them "patience is a virtue" instead. She is rewarding bad behavior.

Likewise, we reward way too much bad behavior from our poli-ticians. I can't tell you how many times I heard during the 2012 Republican presidential primary "anybody but Obama," as if all the candidates were basically the same when nothing could be fur-ther from the truth. Had we learned nothing from the Bush years?

Not to mention, could we possibly raise our standard a little higher than anybody better than arguably the worst, most anti-Constitutional, and anti-Christian president we've ever had? That's like saying "anything but a disembowelment," and settling for having your throat slit. I don't know about you, but instead of debating the least gruesome ways to die I'd rather fight for my life.

On the other hand, as we disciple our friends and neighbors back towards the traditional American view of law and government (i.e. there is a God, our rights come from Him, and government's only purpose/obligation is to defend and secure those God-given rights), we're going to have to learn to reward good behavior which will often come in the form of baby steps. The ruling class and the media and institutions that enable them have institutionalized many of our fellow Americans into a cynical or nihilistic perspective that things can't get any better, thus the best we can hope for is rearranging the deck chairs on the Titanic so we hit the iceberg last. That's exactly what they want you to believe, so that you no longer hold the system to a real standard or demand your elected officials obey their sworn oaths of office.

The idea of real hope and change, not the counterfeit version peddled by Barack Obama, but the kind of real hope and change prevalent at the dawn of American liberty is unrealistic and unattainable to many Americans today. Sadly, that's even true among many conservatives, Libertarians, and Christians.

If we want to spur our neighbors from complacency to conviction, and inspire our fellow patriots to aim higher with their principles, the art of asking questions to spark critical thinking and deconstruct lies and flawed premises is necessary. Most of us are too prideful to be taught by somebody else. Humility is in short supply these days, and I admit I struggle with that, too.

However, if you can rhetorically frame the argument with the right questions so that people come to the right conclusion themselves, then they take ownership of that and internalize it. It becomes *their* belief, not yours. You can lead a horse to water, but you can't make him drink.

Besides, you're not going to be there all the time holding their hand, just like we can't always be there for our kids. If our kids internalize what we've taught them so they take ownership of it, they will act on that even when we're not around. It is the same with our fellow Americans, and especially for our politicians. Conservatives have other priorities higher than government, so we're just never going to be as consistently engaged in the process as the statists that don't. Therefore, it is imperative we support candidates that don't require a lot of babysitting.

Let's use the issue of marriage as an example.

In a culture as divided as ours, it's rare to have a majority on both sides of a debate see something the same way, but it appears as if both a majority of traditionalists (conservatives) and progressives (liberals) have made the same mistake.

As popular culture becomes increasingly aggressive in its promotion of homosexuality, and Americans appear to be more desensitized to it, both sides of the morality debate have taken that as a sign to mean the American people are poised to affirm it. The Left, as well as the increasingly pro-homosexual leadership of the Republican Party, confidently believes the future is on their side. Those of us who believe neither the Bible nor the Constitution are living, breathing documents believe that history is on our side.

Poll after poll shows the American people are clearly more willing to put up with homosexual relationships than they were a few years ago, so how do you explain that at the time this book was being written the pro-marriage forces had won 89% of the elections in which it was contested.

In fact, marriage has even won the day in deep blue states like Oregon. Exit polling found around 40% of Democrats voted for marriage in the swing-state of North Carolina in 2012. On the same day in 2008 when Obama was getting nearly 60% of the popular vote in California and winning Florida, marriage was affirmed by a majority of the very same voters in both states. Despite all the money Obama raised after "coming out" anti-marriage, his poll numbers plummeted. In one 72-hour time span following the 2012 North Carolina marriage vote, Obama lost 9 points in the daily Rasmussen tracking poll, and the dominant issue during that news cycle was marriage.

How do we reconcile all of this seemingly contradictory data?

We do so by recognizing that what we're seeing from the American people isn't a contradiction, but a distinction.

The homosexual movement has done a masterful job of de-stigmatizing those who practice homosexuality as victims of urges they cannot control, but they clearly haven't been as successful at getting the majority of the American people to affirm those same urges as normal and preferable for society.

The American people have on one hand determined they should not stigmatize those practicing homosexuality more or different than they would those immersed in adultery or pornography—thanks mainly to the case the homosexual movement has made that this is hypocrisy (and I agree with them that it is). And about the worst thing to be in today's "tolerant" culture is a hypocrite.

On the other hand, the American people clearly are not ready to normalize homosexual relationships to the point of affirmation or on an equal footing with marriage itself, which explains the 32 election results on the record we have on the issue. I may not be a wannabe political genius like Karl Rove, but even I'm smart enough to recognize a trend after 32 consecutive elections when I see one—especially when that trend crosses geographical and party lines.

A majority of the American people seem to be drawing the same distinction with homosexuality they have drawn with drugs. They're fine with de-criminalizing (or de-stigmatizing) marijuana, but they're also not in favor of outright legalization (affirmation) of narcotics. Many of the Americans who have voted to affirm marriage and not homosexuality still think *Ellen* and *Modern Family* are funny, but they're also not ready to affirm that behavior as normal or preferable.

The same can be said of adultery and premarital sex. Lots of moral traditionalists have for years watched television shows that include characters, even the good guys, engaging in premarital sex or adultery. This may desensitize them on an individual level, but after the show is over they don't tell their children to model that behavior, or want the government schools teaching their kids how to become better adulterers or fornicators.

Furthermore, have you ever noticed that homosexual behavior itself is still not widely portrayed in mainstream pop culture? For example, how often do you see two dudes making out on network television, or two guys waking up next to each other the next morning naked under the sheets—implying they just spent a lust-filled night together—like you do heterosexual couples?

Why is that?

The answer is simple: while the American people have de-stigmatized those practicing homosexual behavior, they have not de-stigmatized or affirmed the behavior itself.

This explains why pop culture propagandists always make sure the most well-adjusted, wise, and well-liked characters in movies and television are homosexuals. They know on a base level most Americans still view the behavior itself on a spectrum ranging from bizarre to repulsive, so homosexuals are depicted much more than homosexuality is.

But what about those polls that show young people will just affirm homosexual relationships as normal when it's their turn to run the culture?

Granted, thanks to Christians allowing the Left unfettered access to indoctrinating the next generation in government schools, the younger generation of Americans is much more affirming of homosexual behavior than perhaps any generation of human beings in human history. However, since at least the 1960s the younger generations have been in favor of legalized drugs and prostitution, and soccer has been the "fastest growing sport" among them as well—but there's little evidence that any of those things are taking over the mainstream anytime soon.

Once folks grow up and have families of their own the natural tendency throughout human history is they become more conservative/traditional. However, we would be wise to not completely count on that with this younger generation, and instead realize right now we have a window to undo the damage done by unchallenged indoctrination and propaganda before it's too late.

And we won't be able to undo that damage if we can't deconstruct the Left's arguments. The best way to perform precision deconstruction is by asking questions. The most lethal question of them all is "why."

Here are some "why" questions that you can use to deconstruct the flawed premises of the Left:

Has anybody ever gotten a job from a poor person? See, all of my jobs came from rich people. So if you say you want to create more jobs than why would you use government to punitively punish the only people capable of creating them?

Are you okay with saying _____ and all his/her children shouldn't be alive? I once asked a panel of those in favor of child killing in some or all situations if they were in favor of killing my friend Rebecca Kiessling, an attorney from Michigan? Kiessling was conceived in rape, and now she's married and has five children. So please understand that when you advocate abortion in these situations you're really saying people like Kiessling, and all of her offspring, shouldn't be alive. The vast majority of pro-child killing individuals will try to quickly change the subject when you put a real face on their death advocacy.

Where do you get off imposing your standard on me? The Left is always the ones saying there's no absolute truth, and none of us has the authority to impose our values or religion on others. So when they want to take the Scriptures completely out of context to justify amnesty or another destined-to-fail big government scheme, you should ask them where they get off imposing their religion on the rest of us? When they call you a bigot for believing in marriage, you should ask them where do they get off imposing their definition of "bigot" on you, and how arrogant are they to presume their definition is even true?

Think about it, even your own kids can fluster you with questions as simple as "why" when they've caught you saying no to something for arbitrary reasons. That's why we parents pull out the old tried and true "because I said so" when we run out of better reasons, or don't have any good ones.

There is power in the "why," especially since most leftists have never been asked why. They've just gotten away with spewing clichés. While we rightfully lament how few conservatives and Christians can actually defend what they believe, the good news is most liberals can't defend theirs as well.

For example, once on my radio program I asked a liberal opposed to marriage and in favor of homosexuality (notice how I don't accept their language or premise when labeling their argument) why we shouldn't go ahead and legalize polygamy as well. After all, if two consenting adults of the same gender can marry each other, why not multiple consenting adults of any gender?

"That's different," he said.

"Why," I asked.

"It just is," he replied.

"But why," I pressed.

"You're arguing apples and oranges," he insisted.

"Why," I repeated. "Why are you discriminating against multiple consenting adults loving each other in a committed relationship at the same time?"

"It's not the same thing," he said, clearly on the defensive now.

"Why," I asked again. "Why would you deny the right to marry to multiple consenting adults?"

He never gave an answer, and it's because his answer wasn't going to be a good one. See, liberals know that most Americans still find polygamy icky, even though pop culture is trying to shove that down our throats now, too. Still, by asking him why he saw a difference between two immoral behaviors each utilizing his same immoral standard, it exposed the fallacy of his entire argument. In other words, I pointed out the same argument he was using for homosexuality can be used for polygamy, an equally immoral but less publicly tolerated behavior at the moment.

The questioning connected the two, and then pointed out that once you strip away all the emotional manipulation and jamming and look at it reasonably and critically, you're really talking about the same immoral and flawed premise Western Civilization has been rejecting for centuries. There is a reason not even ancient Rome, where Nero was said to have once "married" one of his male slaves in the Roman Senate, taught its children homosexuality was a civil sacrament.

Critical thinking people, even immoral pagan ones, reject perpetuating behaviors that work against the perpetuation of their own species.

This is another reason why Americans have wrongly accepted homosexual behavior but rightly rejected redefining marriage. We have allowed the Left to create two separate arguments here, when they're really the same argument. The only reason to stop homosexuals from obtaining a marriage license is because their behavior is immoral. If the behavior is not immoral, then we are practicing discrimination.

The only valid reason to practice discrimination in the Judeo-Christian and American traditions is because someone has violated the agreed-upon moral code and is thus deserving of being discriminated against. Like when we discriminate against felons by denying them their civil rights (free speech, right to keep and bear arms, right to vote, etc.) and put them in prison for their immoral acts.

And no, you don't have the right to have sex with whomever you want. There are people who believe that. We call them rapists.

Anything that requires consent from another person isn't a right. In our system rights are either God-given (unalienable) or guaranteed by the Constitution's limit on government power (like in the Bill of Rights).

There is no right to homosexual sex in the U.S. Constitution. In fact, call up the Constitution on your computer and do a word search for "homosexual" or "same sex" and you'll get zero results. This is all just made up psychobabble by those who oppose everything America is supposed to stand for, all the way down to our own families and the way we perpetuate ourselves.

See what asking "why" opens the door to? When you ask someone whose entire worldview is predicated on subjective emotion and has no defined moral standard "why," you expose their lack of critical thinking as well as the lack of a moral and logical basis for what they believe.

Most Americans, regardless of party affiliation, will reject that level of magical thinking on sight because while they may not be living out *My Utmost for His Highest* in their daily lives, they're probably not living out *Caligula* or "Jerry Springer" either. But the trick is getting the liberals there. "Why" is the rub that lets the genie out of the bottle, and once the genie is out the liberal can't put him back in.

This also works on Republicrats and GOP establishment types. In 2011 I did a radio interview with two Republicrats who claimed to be fiscal conservatives but think "states rights" trumps inalienable rights. I told them governments don't have rights, only individuals do. But I agreed with them that all jurisdiction resides with the states when the Constitution does not specifically grant it to the federal government. However, I also believe no government of any jurisdiction has the "right" to do that which God says is wrong. They disagreed.

"Why do you think that," I asked.

One of the hosts, who clearly had the entire Republicrat talking points memo memorized, came back with, "I just think each state can do whatever it wants. And if one state wants abortion and you're not in favor of it, then move to a state that doesn't have it; and the same with marriage."

"So you want 50 different definitions of what a life and a marriage is," I asked.

"If that happens so be it," he responded.

"I've got to wonder if you've ever read the Constitution," I replied. "Because it includes a 'faith and full credit clause' that demands each state recognize the others' legislation and public records. So what happens when two dudes get married in one state where it's 'legal' and then move to another state where it's not? They decide to get divorced in the state they live now, which doesn't accept their definition of marriage, so the dudes sue that state in federal court under the faith and full credit clause of the Constitution, which may provide a judge a chance to make every state have to accept a new definition of marriage. You just said you didn't want one moral standard imposed from the Feds on all the states, and now your solution would do exactly that."

Then I moved in for the kill.

"Not to mention you'd like 50 different definitions of what a life is. So some states would kill babies, and other states would not. How does an unborn baby killed in one state move to access his right to life in another state? There once was a group of Americans who thought despite what the 5th Amendment to the U.S. Constitution says each state could decide for itself what a human life is, and devalue it if they want to. Maybe you heard of them. They were called Confederates. Congratulations, you think you've latched on to some new, exciting idea but it was already rejected in this country like 150 years ago."

Let's just say the interview didn't last very long after that.

If America's culture war was like a trial, we would be the only ones being cross-examined. We get called to the witness stand and perpetually peppered with skeptical and hostile questioning from the other side's counsel. I'm not complaining about that because that's fair game. But what's not fair is that the other side rarely, if ever, faces the same. Some of that is the dreaded media bias/double-standard we're all aware of and complain about constantly.

But a lot of times that's our own fault as well.

Why do we always feel the need to respond to every red herring disguised as a question from the other side? Why do we always feel compelled to accept and entertain all their flawed premises? Why don't we ever respond to their provocative questions with questions of our own? Most of our fellow Americans know why the Left dislikes our belief system, but on the other hand don't really know what the Left wants to do instead. In today's world of new technologies and social media making it easier than ever to get our message out, we have no one to blame for that but ourselves.

There is power in the "why." Why don't we ask the other side of the debate "why" more often? Why don't we make them defend their belief system at least as much as we have to defend our own?

We won't win until we do.

10

Stay On Message

In 2010 Christine O'Donnell was a national Tea Party darling.

In a year of Republican primary upsets, she had pulled off one of the most unlikely ones. She was being hailed by Sarah Palin and Rush Limbaugh, and being pilloried by all the right people. Her opponents, Democrat and Republican establishment alike, were becoming hysterical in their attempts to discredit her.

One of those hysterical attacks was an old clip of O'Donnell as a young woman on uber-liberal Bill Maher's program admitting to "dabbling" in witchcraft.[83] Countless young people dabble in the occult. Before I became a Christian I was intrigued by it as a youth myself.

For decades pop culture has churned out occult themed television shows and movies targeted at young people about the same age as O'Donnell was when she said she was curious about it. So it seems a little hypocritical at best for the same American Left

---

83 http://www.youtube.com/watch?v=5iWRw3oZdg4

profiting off of selling young people on the occult, to make the case that falling for their own marketing scheme as a youth disqualifies someone from public office later in life as an adult.

What I just wrote is what O'Donnell should've said in response to these ridiculous attacks, or words to that effect, but she didn't. Instead, she fell into the trap of elevating them to the point of validating them by saying in a much-panned commercial "I'm not a witch."[84]

Game, set, and match.

O'Donnell had gone from superstar to supernova in about a month because her campaign fell for the trap of elevating these attacks to a threat level they didn't deserve.

The Left has its own propaganda methodology that would require a whole other book to discuss. The good news is that book has already been written. It's called *The Marketing of Evil* by David Kupelian, and I would highly recommend it. In his book, Kupelian pulls the curtain back to reveal all of the propaganda techniques deployed by the Left. For the sake of our discussion we're going to take a look at one such technique, because how we respond to it usually goes a long way towards determining whether we win or whether we lose. Just ask Christine O'Donnell.

Attacks in political warfare are like parasites. They usually cannot survive merely on their own, so they need to attach themselves to a host to sustain them. Usually the one being attacked ends up being the host, thus springing the trap.

Look again at the example of Christine O'Donnell. With the exception of Karl Rove on Fox News, most of the negative stories about her were coming from liberal blogs and media that only people who were never going to vote for her anyway consume. They were designed to get O'Donnell to do exactly what she did. Get under her skin, offend her, and/or hurt her feelings enough that she will get off message first of all, and then use her platform to give her opponent's propaganda an audience with her own people second.

The Left sets the trap by baiting you to respond to their silliness in a way that gives them access to your audience. They will hound

---

84 http://www.youtube.com/watch?v=uxJyPsmEask

you and hound you until you do. Depending on your resolve and the intensity of the attacks, it takes some longer than others to wear down. Most of their attacks are not really a story outside of the Left's own enclaves until you respond, and then once you do you've given the media the excuse it's been looking for to really crank up the jamming techniques.

As an aside, the Republican Party establishment is beginning to adopt these tactics more and more in taking on conservatives as well.

Once O'Donnell went on TV with "I'm not a witch" the Left didn't allow her to get a word in edgewise from there, other than replaying the clip of her denying she was a witch until every voter in Delaware was sick of it— including the ones that were still going to vote for her. She had given them the money shot sound bite they were looking for, and they were going to play it on loop until Election Day.

The George W. Bush presidency was often a case study in what *not* to do when it comes to circumventing the progressive propagandists, but during his 2004 re-election campaign Bush didn't make one mistake that went a long way to helping him get re-elected. The Left and the media harped continuously on Bush to admit he made mistakes in Iraq, and to even apologize to the American people, but Bush never did. Had he done so, he might as well have gone over to John Kerry and personally handed him the keys to the White House, because the Left would've hung him with that in every commercial break that fall faster than you can say Swift Boat.

Here's an excerpt from a 2004 column in the *San Francisco Chronicle* that is the epitome of what I'm talking about:[85]

There comes a time in every raw dumb imperfect beleaguered human's life when he has to face the music and pay the piper and fess up to his or her crimes and misdemeanors and blatant careening flubs and heartless gaffes and whoa where the hell was my brain that time sorry sorry sorry.

---

85 Mark Morford, "Why Won't Dubya Apologize?" *San Francisco Chronicle,* April 21, 2004, http://www.sfgate.com/entertainment/morford/article/Why-Won-t-Dubya-Apologize-Botched-9-11-info-2790704.php

We all do it. We all smack our palms to our foreheads and trip on our own ideological shoelaces, and we are exasperating and thoughtlessly cruel without knowing it, running roughshod over our noble or ignoble intentions on a daily basis because, well, we are just wired this way.

But then comes the hard part: we apologize. Profusely and maybe even a bit meekly, we ask for forgiveness or at least offer an olive branch and recognize our shared messy humanness as the thing that differentiates us from the saccharine sexless drone people of the world—like, you know, Laura Bush. Shudder.

But then there's Dubya. He is, apparently, immune. He is perfect and flawless and without the slightest taint of guilt or error, and, despite looking like a bowl of Jell-O salad in a universe of divine tiramisu, he is, apparently, an angel of purity and light. It's true.

For here is Dubya, mumbling his way through another shockingly insulting news conference just recently, screwing up both his face and his intelligence data (again) as reporter after reporter asks him, point blank, why he won't simply come clean. They ask him, repeatedly, why he cannot find a single mistake in any policy his slithery administration has unleashed upon the nation, much less confess to any rampant missteps and botched decisions and oily ulterior motives and blatant screw-ups regarding 9/11 and Saddam and WMDs and his fetish for warmongering and for rewriting intelligence data to suit his corporate needs, all while taking more vacations than any president in history.

George W. Bush had many faults as a leader, several of which we've already discussed, but a lack of empathy wasn't one of them. If anything, he was too sensitive to the needs of others and that got him in most of his policy trouble . Under Bush "compassionate conservatism" really just meant pretending as if the Constitution has a "good ideas" provision or a "something must be done" clause when it has neither. The Left was clever in trying to use Bush's empathy against him by daring him to apologize, but Bush's discipline in restraining himself from taking the bait was vital.

After all, do the liberal media capable of writing such sophomoric tripe and calling it a newspaper column strike you as the forgiving type when it comes to conservatives? O'Donnell's campaign didn't have the same restraint, and the Left hoisted her from her own petard.

Goldilocks from the fairy tale *The Three Bears* is a good example to follow when responding to political attacks. Goldilocks tries the first bowl of porridge and it was too hot, and then the second one was too cold, but the third one was "just right."

Translation: you neither want to blow up your opponent's attack nor blow it off. You want to respond in kind (just right). If someone rips you in the comment's section of your buddy's blog that 10 people read, don't blow it up in front of your 500 Facebook friends with short attention spans. Respond in kind on the platform they attacked you with or don't respond at all.

If you're in leadership, or aspire to be, this would be a good time to note the thin line between insulation and isolation. Isolation creates a bunker mentality when we become thin-skinned and see enemies everywhere. But good leaders are insulated to a point from criticism and scrutiny. It's not that they don't hear it, but it's little more than "hey batter swing" chants like they heard when playing Little League baseball back in the day. It's just background noise. They're aware of it enough to know what's going on and to make sure they don't develop a tin ear, but they focus on the big picture because they're confident in the courage of their conviction.

Like in *Star Wars* during the assault on the first Death Star, when Luke Skywalker is distracted by all the cannons and explosions going on around him, and is encouraged to "stay on target."

If you want to stay on target, there are six things you need to remember.

1. All the damage from a contrived attack is self-inflicted. If you avoid the trap, attacks become excellent opportunities. As you read earlier in this book, the only damages that come from being attacked are self-inflicted—either because the attack was true or your response was insufficient. Otherwise an attack gives you a platform to restate your case/mission statement/objective/policy.

The final *Fox News* debate before the 2011 Iowa Straw Poll was billed as a playoff game between battling Minnesotans Michele Bachmann and Tim Pawlenty. Sensing he needed to score big after embarrassingly backing down to Mitt Romney in a previous debate, Pawlenty decided to go after Bachmann this time. Which is a little bit like picking on the captain of the cheerleading squad since you can't beat up the quarterback of the football team.

Except this cheerleader was no shrinking violet.

Pawlenty went right after Bachmann in the debate, trying to show voters she wasn't ready for primetime. Instead of wilting on the one hand or emotionally lashing out on the other, Bachmann kept her cool and treated Pawlenty's desperate attack as an opportunity to finish him off. Forty-Eight hours later Bachmann won the highest voter turnout Iowa Straw Poll ever, and Pawlenty was out of the presidential race.

2. Never argue down unless you can turn it to your advantage. When someone sends me a negative note on social media, I will check to see how many friends they have on Facebook or how many Twitter followers they have before responding. If they have about as many or more than me, I will try to respond if for no other reason than to get access to their platform. If I have substantially more than them, I will ignore them unless there's a chance to take their attack to my audience and use it as a hook (reason) to justify restating my message.

The same goes for radio shows and/or websites that attack me. If they're bigger or on the same scale as me, I take advantage of the opportunity. If they're not, they don't matter and are probably just trying to instigate me giving them access to my platform. Now, if the attack from someone with a smaller platform is so over the top that it fulfills every stereotype I'm constantly warning my audience about so I can use it to my advantage, then I will bring it to their attention because it's like a hanging curve ball just begging to be hammered over the fence.

The one exception is if the attack manages to make its way to your friends/peers/audience/constituents, and you start hearing a lot of feedback from the people that matter most to you. If that's the case then you may need to respond in those situations because your credibility and/or team morale could be at stake.

3. Respond in kind. Our tendency in these moments is to escalate hostilities when threatened, or maybe I'm the only one that struggles with that? Regardless, unless there's an advantage to be gained by escalating hostilities, respond to attacks in kind. Meaning, if someone attacks you on Twitter in 140 characters or less, don't respond with a 2,000-word blog you then email out to everyone on your list.

If you're in public office and you get a handful of nasty emails from constituents angry that you're actually a principled conservative, don't call up the popular local conservative radio host with a much bigger audience and ask to come on his program to respond. Just respond back to those individual constituents in an email like they sent you if you think the dialogue could be productive. Or kick the dust off your sandals and move on, because often it's not who you think it is. The Left has mastered the art of spamming our political and business leaders with emails that read like they're from their local constituents/customers, when they're really all from two guys living together in Hawaii who enjoy Mai Tais and *Will and Grace* reruns.

In 2012 someone wrote an absolutely dishonest blog at *Townhall.com,* where I am also a contributor, attacking the personhood movement as not being pro-life. Instead of defensively blasting it out to their entire list and giving this writer a chance to put doubts in the minds of their own people, which is what these sorts of parasitic attacks want you to do, Personhood USA worked with me to respond with their own piece at *Townhall.com*[86] that rebutted every one of her points.

4. The rule of three. There is a story in the Old Testament of a leader named Nehemiah that God charged with rebuilding the

---

86 Steve Deace, "Personhood is Pro-Life Principles in Action," *Townhall,* June 30, 2012, http://townhall.com/columnists/stevedeace/2012/06/30/personhood_is_prolife _principles_in_action/page/full

walls of his civilization. As soon as Nehemiah went about God's work of doing exactly that, the haters and hypocrites showed up trying to get him to come down to their level and talk each other to death.

They wanted to distract Nehemiah from doing the real work he was called to do, and engage them by pondering the lint in their navel instead. The same thing still happens nowadays. Whatever walk of life you have influence in, if you start taking a stand for righteousness and liberty you can rest assured the haters and hypocrites will want to distract you from working and get you to keep talking to and/or about them instead.

In our more technologically advanced age, that looks like endless streams of back-and-forth Facebook posts or in the comments section of your favorite political website. That's why I generally believe in the rule of three. If I can't settle a dispute in a maximum of three exchanges, then this person either requires someone smarter than me or has ulterior motives. Either way, time to move on.

We only have so much time and energy, so we would be wise to plow the field that might actually yield a harvest. Not to mention the fact incessant engaging of haters and hypocrites makes it harder for us to be the happy warriors that rally others to our side when we let them irritate us.

5. Know your audience. I can't tell you how many phone calls I've gotten over the years from friends of mine in politics wondering how to respond to an attack from a source their supporters would never even look at, let alone take seriously. If you can't respond to an attack in a way that will reach an audience you want/need to reach, or allow you to perpetuate your message in a productive manner, then don't respond at all.

6. There is power in the name. I typically don't believe in responding to anonymous, because it makes us look foolish to get all worked up about what someone with the handle "crackpipe4ever" or "cougartroll" has to say.

If someone doesn't have the guts to put their name on their own words, they never merit a response. And when I say never, I mean never. I believe in this so strongly that for the past several years I have not allowed anonymous authors on my website (except for a soldier blogging for us from Afghanistan, whose identity we kept a secret for obvious reasons), nor do I refer to anything written anonymously.

Furthermore, I don't use pseudonyms for a byline on anything I say, post, or write, and whenever possible nor should you. In a culture of soft-headed metrosexuals like ours, there is real power in a willingness to take a stand and own it. It's like saying, "That just happened—now what are you going to do about it?" Americans have always cherished such bravado, provided it doesn't cross over into egoism.

Most of our opponents are bullies, and most bullies become cowards once you stand up to them. We should be proud of what we believe, because what we believe is true and transforms lives and entire civilizations for the better. There is no reason to hide behind a moniker. You're not Sir Thomas More writing under a pen name to escape execution from overzealous Protestant reformers, or the Founding Fathers using pseudonyms to avoid the Red Coats dragging you off to the gallows. Granted, on the path we're currently on the day may come when that is true, but today is not yet that day. And that day may never come if we're willing to boldly stand up for what we believe.

As patriots we should be as confident in the integrity of our principles as the great Charles Spurgeon was of the integrity of the Bible when he said, "I should no more defend the Bible than I would defend a caged lion. Simply let the lion out of its cage, and it will defend itself just fine."

11

Play Offense

The great Yogi Berra said it best: "Half of this game is 90% mental."

The inconvenient truth is we conservatives are so used to being marginalized that we're often mentally pistol-whipped before the battle even begins. We are so desperate for cultural acceptance that we'll latch on to even the slightest homage to conservativism from a famous figure, no matter how flawed.

In football it is known as a "helmet game," when one team has such a mental stronghold on its rival that the minute things don't go as planned on the field they start collectively thinking to themselves "here we go again" anticipating the worst. When a team has reached that mental breaking point against its rival, it's time for a culture change and that starts by hiring leaders (coaches) who will challenge the status quo and get the players to believe in themselves again.

I think American conservatism is in the exact place my favorite college football team was in back in 1969 when a young coach named Bo Schembechler arrived on the scene from Miami of Ohio. Michigan was built on a winning tradition, just like conservatism, but had fallen behind because the nice guy coach was getting run over by the Buckeye bully Woody Hayes. The final game Michigan played before Schembechler arrived was against Ohio State for the Big Ten championship in 1968, and the Wolverines lost, 50-14.

That's right, despite the fact both teams were ranked in the top 5 the final score was a lopsided 50-14. In order to score 50 points, Ohio State put its starters back in the game for a two-point conversion late in the fourth quarter. When asked afterwards why he went for two points to run up the score on his rival, the brash Ohio State coach said unapologetically "because I couldn't go for three."

Enter Bo Schembechler.

Schembechler had been a Woody Hayes disciple, playing for Hayes and then serving as one of his top assistant coaches at Ohio State. Despite a successful tenure at Miami of Ohio, local media in Detroit asked the question "Bo Who?" when he was hired. The University of Michigan was the Haight-Ashbury of the Midwest in 1969, so it was a bit of culture shock to see this conservative bull in a china shop with a crew cut arrive on campus.

The first thing Schembechler did was purge his program of the soft-headed and uncommitted. That first spring practice was so tough that several players quit. Future NFL Hall of Famer Dan Dierdorf was on that team, and told the media "the track team runs less than us and their coach is nicer."

Schembechler was looking for players willing to do what it took to be great, not pretty good. At a program that had been as successful as Michigan's it's very easy for complacency to set in. Woody Hayes may have had a few faults, but complacency wasn't one of them. He was frankly hungrier than "that school up north" he hated. Meanwhile, Michigan was content to rest on past laurels until Schembechler arrived.

Come fall Schembechler's first season initially got off to a bit of a rocky start with a blowout loss at home to Missouri, and a road loss at Michigan State. But by the time the Wolverines hosted undefeated and top-ranked Ohio State in the season finale in late November, they had jelled as a team and could clinch a Big Ten championship with an upset over the Buckeyes, who were three touchdown favorites.

The talk all season after each Buckeye blowout is where the squad stood in the annals of college football. Analysts at the time said the only team that could beat Ohio State was the NFL's Minnesota Vikings and their famous "purple people eaters."

No one gave this rag-tag bunch of Wolverines much of a chance, and why should they? They had lost by 36 points to these same Buckeyes one year ago. But by the end of that afternoon Michigan pulled off what the pundits called "the upset of the decade," beating Ohio State 24-12. Years later, when a now-retired Woody Hayes reminisced at a banquet about the best team he ever had, the Hall of Fame coach said it was that 1969 team that was upset by Michigan.

That win set the stage for a dominant era of Michigan football. Sixteen of the 21 teams Schembechler coached finished in the top 10 of the final rankings, and he won 13 Big Ten championships. Several coaches under his tutelage went on to have magnificent coaching careers like Hall of Famers Lloyd Carr and Don Nehlen, and national champion coaches Bill McCartney and Les Miles. Schembechler changed a complacent culture and rebuilt it on the pillars of integrity, accountability, and excellence. His leadership helped create other equally successful leaders who put their own spin on Schembechler's vision.

I tell you all of this for two reasons. One, I might be the world's biggest Michigan fan and look for any opportunity to represent for the maize-and-blue, but you could care less about that. Two, because for all the talk of our need for another Ronald Reagan, I think what we really need are some Schembechlers.

There is a fine line between tradition and nostalgia. Tradition is the assurance that you have the right ethics and institutions to be successful again based on what was done in the past, provided you have the right people in place to exploit them. Tradition spurs action and innovation to build upon a foundation of success.

On the other hand, nostalgia is a paralyzing force because it tempts you to keep trying to recreate the precise conditions that led to a specific past success. Often that specific success was a moment in time, and the attempt to repeat it creates a myopic inflation of that success to the point it stalls progress towards a new era of success. Instead of moving forward, you keep trying to go back to the good old days.

Right now we are mired in nostalgia at the expense of our tradition.

We are mired in nostalgia because our entire movement has been defined by one man's success, as opposed to the timeless traditions he fought for. As a result, every sort of Republican now claims Ronald Reagan as their legacy, even the absolute worst ones that might as well be Democrats. A pretty good rule of thumb is that if everybody can claim something, then nobody can.

Yes, Reagan was a gifted man, and I've used several examples of that giftedness in this book. But that giftedness doesn't matter to us if it's not used to advance the principles we hold dear. There have been gifted people throughout history that used their gifts to do wicked and awful things. Why don't we celebrate them? Because what they stood for was wrong or evil, that's why. In other words, what they stood for overshadowed their giftedness.

The same should be true of Reagan's positive legacy as well.

While it's a testimony to his legacy that we still play clips of Reagan to defend our values today, it's also an indictment of how stale we are. At the time I was writing this book I just turned 40 years old. When Reagan first ran for president in 1976 I was still eating paste and my boogers. When Reagan left the White House in 1989 I was in the 10th grade. The emerging generation of conservatives/Libertarians behind me don't remember him at all. Al Gore had yet to invent the Internet. Cell phones were a hand-held monstrosity for the rich. There was no DirecTV. We hadn't even invented those really cool frozen yogurt places where you buy in bulk depending on the amount of toppings you have. Heck, MTV was still playing music videos back then!

You know how ancient the "Macarena" seems now? Well, when

Reagan left office the Macarena was still eight years away from splitting our ear drums, and we still didn't know "who let the dogs out" as well.

The distance between 1989 and now is made even longer by how quickly information is transmitted with all our technology nowadays. When Reagan left office we were just beginning the era of the 24-hour news cycle. Now we have the 24-minute news cycle (if you take out the commercials) in 140 characters or less on Twitter. Quoting Reagan to the emerging generation today is like quoting Calvin Coolidge. Another great conservative, mind you, but they don't remember him, either.

It's time to move forward. Notice I didn't say move on, but move forward. Moving on either means forgetting the past or casting it aside. Moving forward means honoring it, and then building on it. We don't need to return to the era of Reagan anymore than the Democrats need to return to the era of FDR. What we need to do is take the success Reagan had and build on it while at the same time learning from his failures. That's how you move forward.

And yes, Reagan had failures. He wasn't a perfect angel that tip-toed through the raindrops without getting wet. That's nostalgia talking.

Back to my beloved Michigan Wolverines for a second. After a phenomenal 40-year run, the university administration decided to move on from the Schembechler era rather than move forward. So they brought in Rich Rodriguez as head coach in 2008, and in the span of just three years his tenure nearly dismantled five decades worth of a foundation that had been built. Rodriguez lost as many Big Ten games in his three seasons in Ann Arbor as Michigan had lost the previous 12 seasons combined.

Rodriguez was eventually replaced by Brady Hoke, who was a part of the Schembechler era. Hoke returned Michigan to its Schembechler-era pillars, but moved forward at the same time. He's not running the same offense and defense Schembechler was running in 1969. He's not prickly with the media the way Schembechler was early in his career, but instead realizes the necessity of being professional and available with the media telling your story to future recruits. He runs a contemporary program built on the foundation of a timeless tradition. In his first season in 2011 he went 11-2, ended a 7-year losing streak to Ohio State, and notched Michigan's first major bowl victory in 12 years. That's what I call moving forward.

The debate isn't about who is the next Reagan. The debate is about whether to move on or move forward from the Reagan era. Right now the Republican Party on national level is run by those who would rather move on. Sure, they use Reagan in their branding and fundraising, but they're far removed from the bold colors Reagan stood for. Their uniform is pale pastels.

What I suggest we do is move forward. Reagan won two big arguments with the Left—low taxes spur economic growth, and peace through strength (forcing the collapse of the Soviet Union via the arms race). Even Democrat presidents nowadays when they're in trouble offer targeted tax cuts and tax rebates as a means to spur economic development. So the debate is no longer about whether or not to cut taxes, but for whom and by how much.

In addition, the era of the dovish Democrat president is over. President Clinton set a record for the most military deployments. President Obama may have talked a good George Soros game when running for president in 2008, but his foreign policy is virtually indistinguishable from his Republican predecessor (for better or for worse), and he's very proud to be the commander-in-chief that got Osama bin Laden. That's a far cry from Democrats in the 1980s feting communist Sandinista leader Daniel Ortega at beltway cocktail parties.

However, Reagan failed to substantially reduce the size of government, did nothing substantive to dismantle the Left's monopoly on education (and as Abraham Lincoln said "he who controls the classroom in this generation will run the government in the next"), lent his name to a failed amnesty program that turned California from red to blue in elections for the last two decades, and appointed two mediocre-to-terrible Supreme Court justices.

We don't need to keep having arguments we've already won. We need to start winning arguments we haven't yet had. It's time to stop pining away for the salad days and move forward and build on Reagan's legacy. Not settle for it. The Reagan era was supposed to be the vanguard of a conservative Renaissance, and instead it became the high water mark.

Kobe Bryant and Lebron James were instantly compared to Michael Jordan coming into the NBA. Both of them initially did little to temper those comparisons, and early on they each languished under the sheer weight of them. It wasn't until they became their own men (James had to move to another team to make that happen) and developed their own games that both became repeat champions.

If we truly want to honor Reagan's legacy, we must stop drowning in nostalgia awaiting his heir apparent, and instead rally around the principles he fought for. While we keep trying to turn the clock back, the Left keeps moving forward.

It's time for a new generation of leadership that combines a respect for tradition with a hatred for losing, and that means losing in the public policy arena and not just on Election Day. A new generation eager to prove themselves like Schembechler was when he arrived at Michigan in 1969, and willing to get rid of the dead weight and not accept good as good enough when only greatness will do.

It's time for leaders that aren't here to make friends with the system, but have a cause they believe is worth fighting and dying for if necessary. Leaders who don't create followers that become groupies or hanger-ons or lifelong political hacks, but instead inspire others to themselves become leaders that move on and take the fight elsewhere when they're ready.

We've got too many people comfortable with losing not as bad and calling it a win. We need leaders from the Ricky Bobby motivational school who understand "second place is the first loser."

And in our case winning isn't simply winning an election, but winning the future for our children and grandchildren.

We need a house cleaning and a culture change. We need to hit the control-alt-delete buttons and reboot. You do that when your computer itself is still in good shape, but is locked up and not working the way it should. Similarly, our principles are still good, but the process of implementing them and advancing them has lockjaw.

We have already discussed in this book how too often we accept the Left's premise and allow them to have the moral high ground, so too often we end up being defined by what we're against and not what we're for. We also have failed to define what it is we're actually conserving as conservatives, which is an inherent weakness of our movement that 19th century theologian R.L. Dabney presciently observed:

> (Conservatism's) history has been that it demurs to each aggression of the progressive party, and aims to save its credit by a respectable amount of growling, but it always acquiesces at last in the innovation. What was the resisted novelty of yesterday is today one of the accepted principles of conservatism; it is now conservative only in affecting to resist the next innovation, which will tomorrow be forced upon its timidity and will be succeeded by some third revolution; to be denounced and then adopted in its turn. American conservatism is merely the shadow that follows Radicalism as it moves forward towards perdition. It remains behind it, but never retards it, and always advances near its leader.

Every time I read that quote it never fails to hit too close to home.

As a Christian I am commanded in the Bible to always have "a ready defense" for my faith, but nowhere am I commanded to remain perpetually on the defensive. The Gospel itself is an offensive action. The result of a sovereign God who does not sit passively by like a kid with an ant hill as His creation goes to pot, but instead actively engages His creation to the point of coming to earth Himself to reach out to us flesh-to-flesh. The American Revolution was also an offensive action, with patriots taking action to preserve their God-given rights.

I don't want to conserve the Left's agenda, by growing government less than they would, killing fewer children than they would, and destroying marriage incrementally through civil unions instead of outright handing over the institution of marriage like they would. I want to defeat the Left, not conserve it. When it's time for my generation to leave the world stage, I want us to be known as the generation that did to America's Leftist Progressives what Reagan did to the Soviet Union.

To make that happen we need to play offense.

Offense is essential, because you have to be on offense to score points, and you have to score points to win. Playing offense also boosts your side's morale while doing psychological damage to the other side. Go back to the beginning of this chapter when I talked about how mentally beaten down we are. That's purely the result of the perception the Left is always on the offensive and we're always on the defensive. That's why there's so much talk about returning to the Reagan era today, because other than the early days following the 1994 Republican takeover of Congress that really was the only time any of us can remember our side on the offensive.

I think that's also one of the reasons the late Andrew Breitbart made such an impact on the conservative movement despite passing away at only 43 years old, which is an age when most men are just starting to come into their own. Breitbart played offense and went after the Left, and was equipping others to do the same.

The Left's confidence has morphed into hubris because they're used to playing offense, and we've conditioned them to anticipate our surrender any minute now. That's why when one of our people does play offense it really throws them into a hissy fit.

A good example of this was something Kentucky Senator Rand Paul did during the summer of 2012. Yes, *that* Rand Paul. The one who stepped in it earlier in this book. This time he stepped *on* it, or rather, them.

To do Rand justice, let's quote directly from the story the liberal *Huffington Post* did on the example I'm citing:

Sen. Rand Paul (R-Ky.) moved this week to hold a noncontroversial flood insurance bill hostage until the Senate agrees that life begins at fertilization.

The bill, which would financially boost the National Flood Insurance Program on the cusp of hurricane season, had been expected to pass easily in the Senate. But since Paul on Monday offered an unrelated "fetal personhood" amendment, which would give legal protections to fetuses from the moment of fertilization, Senate Majority Leader Harry Reid (D-Nev.) is threatening to halt progress on the legislation.

"I'm told last night that one of our Republican senators wants to offer an amendment—listen to this one—wants to offer an amendment on when life begins," Reid said on the Senate floor Tuesday. "I am not going to put up with that on flood insurance. I can be condemned by outside sources; my friends can say, 'Let them have a vote on it.' There will not be a vote on that on flood insurance. We'll either do flood insurance with the amendments that deal with flood insurance, or we won't do it. We'll have an extension."

*Reid has allowed Republicans to attach unrelated amendments to other important bills in the past few months. **But Reid called Paul's measure "ridiculous" and "outlandish," and asked Republicans to deal with him on "their side of the aisle."***

Now *that's* the kind of leadership I'm talking about.

Rand Paul played offense by attaching personhood (the ultimate pro-life principle in action) onto a bill that was expected to pass easily. By doing so he would either force the Democrats to give him his vote on it, or cause them to make total fools out of themselves as Reid does in this article. Like when Reid expresses incredulity that we would actually debate something as trite and insignificant in the U.S. Senate as "when life begins." Given that life is one of the unalienable rights to life posited in our founding document, is there anything more important for our elected officials to be debating?

I put that part of the *Huffington Post* story and a few other lines in bold for a reason, because they're examples how by Rand Paul playing offense we have grabbed the moral high ground and are making the Left accept our premise.

Note the article doesn't refer to Rand's pro-life bill as "anti-Reproductive freedom" but as "personhood." If they're going to report accurately on the bill, even the liberal *Huffington Post* has to use that term because personhood isn't having an argument with anti-lifers about how many kids we're going to permit them to kill, or how we'll let them kill them, or when we'll let them kill them after they jump through a few hoops (i.e. "and then you can kill the baby"). Personhood is a debate about whether or not all life is precious and sacred. Personhood *is* the high ground.

Rand Paul got the Democrat Senate Majority Leader to call debating when life begins "ridiculous" and "outlandish." Remember the 2008 presidential forum hosted at Saddleback Church when Rick Warren asked Barack Obama, "at what point does a (unborn) baby deserve human rights?" Remember Obama's flippant "that's above my pay grade" response? Remember that was one of the few times you actually thought John McCain could win the election? That's because it was about the only time in the entire campaign that McCain grabbed the moral high ground and played offense— with a considerable assist from Warren's question.

Rand Paul managed to do something here few pro-life politicians have successfully been able to do for years: get the Left off script and reacting to our argument. Reid is so frustrated with what Rand Paul did here he insisted Republicans deal with him "on their side of the aisle." If a committed pro-life Republican wanted to challenge Reid in his next election, they've got one whale of a sound bite to use against him now.

The Republican leadership in the U.S. Senate—and everywhere else for that matter—should be constantly emulating what Rand Paul did here. The real question is how come Rand Paul in his second year in the U.S. Senate managed to get under Reid's skin in a way most of the Republicans who have been up there for eons haven't?

Rand did something else by doing this as well—he boosted team morale. Maybe it's a coincidence Rand did this just two weeks after his endorsement of establishment proxy Mitt Romney drew the ire of many of his supporters, but before we become too cynical we should note the first bill Rand Paul ever sponsored as a U.S. Senator was a personhood bill, so while the timing may not be a coincidence it's clear this is a principle that Rand cares deeply about.

By playing offense with his principles, Rand changed the conversation from his lackluster endorsement to his bold leadership. He didn't undo all the damage he did to his base with this one gesture, but he took a giant first step towards doing so.

Not to be outdone, Senator Ted Cruz has produced a highlight reel of similar moments early in his first term as a U.S. Senator. As a result, there is more excitement for Cruz among the grassroots than any Republican politician I can remember, and it's because he's seen as someone that can play offense whether it's a confirmation hearing, taking the fight to the Left, or confronting Republicrats like John McCain on the floor of the U.S. Senate.

As one mainstream media reporter told me off the record: "Cruz is a different animal. You ask a lot of these other Republicans a question that requires an answer other than their talking points, and they stall or look to change the subject. Cruz comes right after the question, turns it around on the questioner if he doesn't like it, and then always has an answer ready to go if he does."

This is why I told *National Review* last year that Cruz isn't just a potential 2016 GOP presidential candidate. He's a force of nature. I'm too young to remember the ascendancy of Reagan, but in my lifetime nobody has better articulated the principles of the conservative grassroots on a national level than Cruz. Throw in his family's powerful testimony as first-generation immigrants escaping tyranny and he has the total package it takes to take on the ruling class.

Leadership always wins, and people love a winner.

Remember the mantra of the Republicrats: "Surrender now, before it's too late." The GOP and sadly many conservatives are punch drunk, believing on one hand the majority of the country is with us while at the same time walking around with the proverbial Sword of Damocles dangling over our heads. Conservatives long for a day when America suddenly wakes up and returns to her Constitutional republican roots, but it's hard to do that when conservatives rarely attempt to advance their principles beyond their own enclaves and subcultures.

"Wacko birds" like Rand Paul, Ted Cruz, and Mike Lee of Utah aren't waiting until there's a Republican majority to push their moral convictions, or waiting for any other harmonic convergence which never occurs that the Republicrats say we must have before we can actually play offense with our principles. They're acting instead as someone that believes they're accountable to conscience, convictions, and constituents—not the corrupt process or some phony definition of Senate collegiality.

During parts of campaign 2012 I was a frequent guest on MSNBC, and just about every time I announced I was going to go on a fellow conservative would either email or tweet me that I should never go on that channel because of its liberal leanings. Yet on MSNBC I've had the opportunity to take some of the most hard-right positions on issues you'll see anywhere on national television, and even share my Christian testimony.

In fact, I once received the following email from Jonathan Collegio, who is the communications director for Karl Rove's American Crossroads:

I've been meaning to reach out for a while - not regarding the conservatives v. Rove sideshow, but because I wanted to thank you for giving some of the best, most fearless and most succinct remarks on the Gospel I've heard on TV, ever. I can't remember exactly when it was, but I remember it was in the MSNBC and I suddenly looked up from my desk and saw you basically preaching the good news about Jesus to Tamron Hall and the other guests as they kind of stood there, stunned. It was likely the most gospel centered message ever given on MSNBC, and I just wanted to tell you how much I appreciated it. God has blessed you with great communication skills, and it encouraged me to see you be so boldly talking about Jesus - especially in the face of an audience like that.

Last I checked, if you want to govern you have to win a majority of the hearts and minds of the voters. To win a majority of those hearts and minds at some point means we're going to have to venture into foreign territory with the courage to engage them. That's how we generate converts.

St. Paul changed entire cultures with nothing more than the Word of God and a tent-making kit, and he did so under the constant threat of death. The only threat we're under is being mocked or rejected.

Sure, after I go on MSNBC I often get called every nasty name in the book by the tolerance mob. But I've also received several emails from folks who said that because of my willingness to be honest in my analysis (holding Republicans to the same standard as Democrats) and respectful when making my arguments, they're willing to consider what I'm saying when previously they dismissed it. I even had a producer at MSNBC tell me once, "I used to think you were crazy, and I'm still not sure I agree with anything you say. But you actually have facts and figures to back up why you believe what you believe, so at the very least I've come around to understanding how someone could think the way you do."

When Bobby Bowden took over as football coach at Florida State he scheduled road games at places like Nebraska and Michigan to get his team featured on national television. The Seminoles weren't the college football power back then they eventually became, so Bowden had to accept one-game contracts with no return game in Tallahassee. Still, Bowden decided the exposure for the Florida State brand was worth the risk. That plan eventually paid off. The Seminoles increased exposure to their brand and were able to recruit better players as a result. Those players eventually helped them win some of those road games, and Florida State eventually set a record by finishing in the top 5 of the final AP college football poll a record 14 consecutive seasons. Bowden eventually surpassed his legendary idol Bear Bryant in all-time wins as well.

We have the truth and tradition on our side, meaning that human history proves our principles are true. Every society that has embraced the ideology of the Left has been cursed, and every society that has embraced ours has been blessed. It's no coincidence that the more we lurch to the Left the worse off the average American becomes. We should be as confident as Breitbart and Bowden in taking our beliefs and brand out into the culture at-large and playing offense with them. It not only scores points and reaches the unconverted, but it also keeps up the morale of our own troops and rallies the base.

In the 2010 midterm elections we had a great goal-line stand that stopped the Left from shoving Obamacare and Cap & Tax down our throats, which would've been the game-clinching touchdown for the progressives. However, any knowledgeable football fan knows that when your offense gets the ball back after a goal-line stand, you're on your own 1-yard line—with 99 yards to go for you to score a touchdown. Fellow patriot, I believe that is an accurate picture of where we currently stand.

We need to start playing offense, and putting the Leftists on the defensive. Obviously 99-yard touchdown plays are rare, but at the very least we need leaders and arguments that give us some first downs so we can improve our field position. First downs build momentum, and get your crowd back in the game. String together enough first downs, and before you know it you're in position to score a touchdown. And we need touchdowns, not settling for field goals.

We are facing at-best a long generational grind to restore the republic, and the longer we take to go on offense the longer it will take to preserve freedom and liberty for our children and grandchildren.

Take too long and we'll be out of time altogether.

12

Conclusion

For a while now you have suspected your wife hasn't been telling you everything.

She's always cared about her appearance, but lately she's been piling on the makeup like she hasn't since you were dating. She showers a lot, and takes longer lunches. Her text message alert on her phone goes off prompting her to giggle and blush. You ask her what's up, "just a friend saying something funny" she says. You even hear her mumbling another man's name in her dreams at night.

You know in your gut something is amiss. You suspect a betrayal is happening right under your very nose. But you have loyalty to this relationship. Not to mention the fact you don't want to be made to look the fool, and you're scared of what the endgame is should your suspicions prove to be true. This has been the only life you've ever known. If you confront her and she doesn't want to work through the situation, can you handle living life alone? Are you really ready to start dating all over again? Will you ever be able to trust again even if you were?

Not yet ready to wrestle with those questions you decide to punt and kick the can down the road for now. Essentially you decide you would prefer to live a lie rather than confront the potential truth.

Weeks go by and you pretend to be blissfully ignorant, but in the back of your mind the lack of intimacy between you and your wife is starting to really gnaw at you. Especially since you're pretty convinced another man is rubbing your rhubarb. But again, the thought of confronting the truth is just too painful.

Until one day you come home from work early and there's a strange car in your driveway. You unlock the front door and are greeted with awkward noises and moaning coming from upstairs. Your instincts have you climbing the stairs to see what's going on when you really don't want to know. The front door to your bedroom is wide open. You reach the top of the stairs and peak through the doorway, only to witness your wife carrying on with another man in the middle of the day in your own bed.

Shattered you say not a word as you descend to the bottom of the stairs. You walk into the family room, looking out the window pondering your next move. Emotionally you're a mixture of anger, revolt, and defeat. All of a sudden you hear the refrigerator door open in the kitchen. But before you walk over to see who it is, you are confronted with the image of a naked man drinking one of your favorite beverages walking right past you like it's nobody's business. He doesn't even acknowledge you're there while he sits down in your recliner and leans back to bring the footrest up. He says not a word until he brazenly asks you, "Hey man, do you know where the remote control is?"

This is the point of no return grassroots patriots have reached with the current leadership of the Republican Party.

Ronald Reagan once famously said "I didn't leave the Democrat Party, the Democrat Party left me."

These days, millions of grassroots patriots around the country feel the same about a Republican Party seemingly hell-bent on abandoning every principle other than crony capitalism. Recently on Fox News, conservative rock star Sarah Palin channeled that frustration when she said:

> *I love the name of that party—'Freedom Party.' And if the GOP continues to back away from the planks in our platform, from the principles that built this party of Lincoln and Reagan, then yeah, more and more of us are going to start saying, 'You know, what's wrong with being independent,' kind of with that Libertarian streak that much of us have. In other words, we want government to back off and not infringe upon our rights. I think there will be a lot of us who start saying 'GOP, if you abandon us, we have nowhere else to go except to become more independent and not enlisted in a one or the other private majority parties that rule in our nation, either a Democrat or a Republican.' Remember these are private parties, and you know, no one forces us to be enlisted in either party.*

Whenever I'm asked about this, and I'm asked about this a lot, I usually say "I'd like to try a second party before thinking about a third one."

Venting frustration is one thing. Acting upon it is entirely another. When we're frustrated, there are plenty of things we can justify as a response, but many of those things aren't necessarily prudent. That's why we have the saying "cooler heads prevailed."

On the other hand, there is certainly a time and place to fashion a whip of cords or grab the jawbone of an ass and give 'em your best Howard Beale.

So is it time for us to abandon the GOP or continue to try and reform it? Let's do a cost-benefit analysis before deciding.

1. The Vision

Cost—With the light of liberty barely a flicker, the absolute worst use of time for conservatives would be essentially starting over to form a 3rd Party movement that may take decades to realize.

Given how much freedom, liberty, and morality we've lost, our constitutional republic probably doesn't have decades. We need to do as much good as we can, and we need to do it right now.

Benefit—Loyalty to the Republican Party has done nothing to squelch our slouch towards Gomorrah or statism. We've wasted years as it is propping up neo-statists and gutless RINOs, with little to nothing to show for it. Instead of wasting more time on the rotting corpse that is the GOP, better to get to work now on what will inevitably take its place. Short-term thinking is what got us here in the first place.

2. Political Impact

Cost—Leaving the Republican Party would essentially hand almost every election of consequence to the Democrats for the foreseeable future and render conservatives meaningless in the grand scheme of things. Furthermore, if no longer held accountable by conservatives, you'll likely see the Republican Party ruling class openly conspire with Democrats to continue to grow government, which means liberty will be lost even quicker. This rash move would take us quicker to irrelevancy.

Benefit—The Republican Party ruling class is already conspiring with Democrats to grow government, despite our presence. In 2013 they passed the largest tax increase in 20 years, for example. At least if we're no longer covering for these sellouts we can recover some integrity lost by associating with the tarnished GOP brand and perhaps have an honest conversation with the American people about where we're headed for once. By forming a 3rd Party, we become de facto independents, and instead of being taken for granted we become a crucial swing vote.

3. Organization

Cost—Sure, there are days when the idea of bolting the GOP sounds great, but it's just not feasible. The two most viable right-of-center 3rd Parties—the Libertarian and Constitution Parties—still don't have consistent ballot access in all 50 states. Good luck recruiting candidates without ballot access, good luck raising money without candidates, and good luck moving your agenda without money. The reality is the two dominant parties have made this kind of effort almost impossible without an unprecedented fundraising/legal effort to build up to it. I don't like it. I wish that weren't the case, but it is what it is.

Benefit—That was the same argument used against our Founding Fathers when they wanted to declare their independence. If there's anything American history has taught us, it's that when we step out on faith and principle, providence handles the rest. One great way to ignite such an effort is to have leaders with charisma, vision, and integrity lead the way in inspiring others to act on the courage of their convictions. Maybe some of those leaders will emerge if we step out on faith. Founding Fathers like George Washington and Thomas Jefferson became the men we know them as today because they rose to the occasion when history needed them.

4. The Future

Cost—Most of us would agree the party is broken, but let's not throw the baby out with the bath water here. The brokenness of the party reflects the cultural brokenness of the times in which we live. All private organizations are only as good as the people inhabiting them. Any new organization will eventually just develop the same problems the GOP has now. You can't expect a political party to have more moral purity than the culture as a whole. Still, reform is necessary. Instead of reinventing the wheel, why not encourage members of the Constitution and Libertarian Parties to infiltrate the GOP? Many local and state Republican Party organizations across the country are in dire need of people. Who says those people can't be people of principle? Let's do to the GOP from the bottom-up what the progressives already did to the Democratic Party. There's no reason we can't overrun the party's infrastructure and put our own people in there.

Benefit—Some Libertarians tried this, and look what the party bosses did to them at the rules committee meeting prior to the 2012 convention in Tampa. That was Soviet-style politics. Of course you can't expect a private organization to be more righteous than the culture, but that actually proves my point. We are aligned with people who don't share our moral value system and have proven they will do things to beat us they would never do to Democrats. And they'll even use Fox News and other "conservative media" to do it. The time, talent, and treasure wasted on reforming the GOP is like trying to funnel foreign aid for the hungry through a corrupt local warlord. Whatever we send just ends up in his pocket. Let's face it, this whole debate is moot anyway because the party bosses are in the process of betraying us first. Thus the longer we wait, the harder it will be to do what we'll eventually have to go ahead and do anyway.

Now that you've had a chance to weigh the pros and cons of each side of the argument, it's time for you to decide.

I don't know about you, but I don't think this a clear-cut call. In fact, I see compelling evidence for arguments on both sides. But what if I told you that you may not have to choose? That you might be able to have what amounts to a 3rd Party without starting completely over and losing the ground you've already taken?

When I pitched the idea of this book to some friends of mine, they were concerned that the other side would read it and then know our playbook and use it against us. But I explained to them that's not possible, because this attack plan only works with our worldview. The reason you don't see too many Republican leaders using these 10 Commandments of Political Warfare, and we've had to cite several of the same names over and over again as examples of Republicans that do, is because most Republican leaders *can't* use them.

They don't have the worldview to use them, so it wouldn't work for them even if they tried. They'd simply be exposed as posers, for these tactics only work for those with conviction. Thus, they have to resort to tactics that look more in line with what the Left does than what you just read in this book.

If they ever actually deploy any tactics at all. Most of them don't even do that. They simply wait until their soul-less consultants, who are usually dumber than they are, tell them what to think.

If you put the commandments in this book to practical use wherever you have influence, you're going to be able to separate the wheat from the chaff real quick-like. Whether that's at your state legislature, a town hall hosted by your Congressman who's home for recess, your local state party, when you're running for office, or even casual conversation among friends and families. That's one of the things these commandments are meant to do.

For too long we have mistaken "friendlies" for "friends."

"Friendlies" are people you can align with on a temporary basis when your vested interests are mutual, but those aren't long-lasting relationships. As circumstances change your "friendlies" can become your enemies once your vested interests no longer intersect.

"Friends" stick closer than a brother. "Friends" get in a foxhole with you. "Friends" have your back when the going gets tough. "Friends" share your convictions and mission, and although at times you may disagree on how best to carry it out, you're both aiming for the same end goal.

Most of the Republican leaders we have aligned ourselves with are "friendlies" but they are not our "friends." This explains why at times they seem so right on, and at other times so far off. They're so right on when we have a mutually beneficial vested interest, and so far off when we don't. Sometimes they'll shield us from the firing squad aiming for us, and then sometimes they'll join it.

If they were "friends" they'd have the same angst and sense of urgency for our civilization's future that we have. They wouldn't need prodding or pressure to take a stand. We wouldn't have to worry about what will happen the minute we stop hounding them to do the right thing.

Increasingly our "friendlies" have become less and less friendly. But instead of letting our "friendlies" use us, why don't we use them?

Children see things in extremes, but adults draw distinctions. We need to stop having a child-like relationship with the GOP, where we rely on the party to save America and treat its big names like our favorite athletes. "Hey, I'll trade you a Marco Rubio rookie card for a Paul Ryan All-Star!" How ridiculous does that sound? Yet that's often how we've behaved.

Political parties prey on that sort of cult of personality, and encourage it, for it means politics becomes about personalities and not about principles. Personalities are much easier to manipulate. Principled leadership comes with a cost, and often requires sacrifices (lives, fortune, sacred honor) a ruling class would prefer not to make.

We don't owe this party any loyalty. I repeat: we don't owe this party any loyalty. One more time in case you missed it: we don't owe this party any loyalty.

They owe us.

There would've never been a Reagan era to wax nostalgic about if it weren't for us. The Republican Party was going nowhere fast after the Watergate era until the birth of the conservative movement. The Republican Party victories of 2010 were done in spite of the party. They didn't want champions like Ted Cruz, remember? We had to drag them kicking and screaming into the winner's circle.

The Republican Party didn't make us. We made them.

We don't take the orders around here. We give them. Or at least we ought to be. We don't take sanctimonious lectures from our employees about how "half a loaf is better than none" or "the lesser of two evils." We run the show, so we determine what the acceptable standard is, who met that standard, and how to hold them accountable when they don't meet it.

I no longer feel a compulsion to vote for every Republican opposite every Democrat, and I haven't voted straight ticket Republican in years. I came to realize that's the coward's way out. Doesn't mean I'm voting for Democrats, but it does mean I'm also no longer voting for Democrats calling themselves Republicans.

"But Steve," some of you will say, "at least a bad Republican is better than a good Democrat."

If by now you haven't realized that a bad Republican and a good Democrat are one in the same, immediately go back to page one and start re-reading this book.

"But Steve," some of you will say, "in our system majority rules so even a bad Republican will still vote Republican for leadership positions."

So what? Why in the Sam Hill should I care if John Boehner or Nancy Pelosi is the Speaker of the House? Not once, not twice, not thrice, but four times in 2013 Boehner allowed bills to pass out of the House of Representatives a majority of Republicans didn't vote for. Two of those were the largest tax increase in twenty years (the fiscal cliff[87]) and the largest tax increase of all time (Obamacare[88]). What's the point of having a majority then?

At least when Pelosi is giving us failed policies and statism I can blame it on the Democrats, and then recruit good candidates to challenge them in the next election. Bad Republicans are actually *worse* than Democrats in that respect, because they depress the conservative base and make it harder to get our people engaged.

Think about it, are you more eager to take on the perp who breaks into your house and threatens your loyal and loving wife, or the disloyal wife you found out was cheating on you? One situation spurs you to act on your God-given masculine instinct. The other rips your still-beating heart from your chest and demoralizes you.

I agree success in our system is based on building coalitions, but those have to be coalitions of the willing. What is the point in giving "Ditch" McConnell or Lindsey Grahamnesty another six years in the United States Senate? Why would I align myself, even temporarily, with someone who has more in common with Democrats than with me? Especially when they come from red states like Kentucky and South Carolina.

Who cares if the Democrat wins in those sorts of places because they'll be easy to beat in the next election in those states. But let a Republicrat like Ditch McConnell become an entrenched

---

87 Steve Deace, "Dear Washington, Thanks for My New Tax Increase," *USA Today,* January 18, 2013, http://www.usatoday.com/story/opinion/2013/01/18/payroll-tax-increase-debt/1840793/

88 Steve Deace, "Breaking: Obama Routs GOP (Again)," October 16, 2013, http://stevedeace.com/news/national-politics/breaking-obama-routs-the-gop-again/

incumbent Republican and you'll suffer under his gangster government for decades.

See, adults don't need instant gratification. Children do. Adults put off instant gratification because they see the bigger picture. Children get emotionally manipulated to act upon what's best right now without any perspective.

Granted, if a Scott Brown is the best you can do in the bluest of blue states like Massachusetts, so be it. But as groups like Club for Growth and the Madison Project point out, there's no reason not to have a real conservative as the Senator to every red state, and the Congressmen to every red district.

I say we start building from there and then it's easier to keep the squishes of the world like Scott Brown in line once elected, when they're surrounded by a caucus led by the likes of Ted Cruz and not Ditch McConnell.

These are some simple (notice I didn't say easy) steps to actually forging a real opposition party in America again. Before making the decades-long investment in a viable 3rd party, why not try this? We don't have to be mascots for the Republican Party, but simply use the Republican Party as a means to an end when it suits us. I am not talking about reforming the Republican Party, because it's well beyond that now. I'm talking about essentially running a party within a party, and using them the way they've used us for years. And only on our terms.

Stop treating the GOP like a religious cult. Let's re-evaluate our relationship with the party, and make it less personal and more business-like. When your employees don't do the job you hired them to do, you don't feel emotionally betrayed and then close up shop. No, you simply fire them and get better employees. This party isn't deserving of our emotions, nor is it worth the salt in our tears.

And no political party ever has been.

No matter where we go or what we build we'll eventually manifest the same problems. Trust me, I'm an Evangelical. We break up churches and start new denominations all the time, believing that this time we'll get it right. But we forget the problem ultimately is us.

Someone once asked G.K. Chesterton what's wrong with the world. He gave them a one word answer: "me."

Our nature is fallen, as is all of Creation. The Republican Party, or any organization or institution for that matter, is only as good as the people inhabiting it. When we turn a political party into a church, and politicians into angels/demigods, we're asking for the very disappointment we have received.

Render unto Caesar that which is Caesar's, and render unto God that which is God's. Do not give Caesar your conscience or virtue. That alone belongs to God. When Caesar demands either he's demanding you recognize him as God, and we have a simple answer for that.

No.

We don't contort our moral values into a pretzel to justify voting for another Republicrat hack. We demand that Republicrat hack meet our standard for hiring or heaven hath no fury like the next primary cycle.

Speaking of primaries, they are the most immediate route to move the country Right. In many places we in the grassroots outnumber the establishment, so as long as we actively and smartly participate in the primary process replacing these Republicrats is not nearly as hard as we've been led to believe.

But for too long we have ignored the primary process at our own peril. We're now at the point the primary really is the election, for if the wrong kind of Republican wins the primary the general election becomes a moot point. If you're aligned with a conservative or Libertarian organization that isn't willing to take a strong and public stand in primaries then get out now! More than likely they are little more than caretakers for the ruling class, running their own shadow incumbent protection program. Primaries separate the men from the boys. Primaries tell us who's here to really take on the system, and who's here to be a part of the system.

Seriously, I think if we just did those two things—stopped being partisan loyalists and started participating in primaries en masse—we'd be amazed at how much positive change we would see based off that alone. And that's something you can do even if you want to belong to a 3rd party and not be a full-time Republican. Many states allow you to vote in open primaries, or register on the same day as the event. Why not go in and vote for the best Constitutional conservative(s) on the ballot?

Barack Obama is correct about one thing. We are the people we've been waiting for. Change for the better is not going to come from the top-down beginning in Washington, D.C. Change is only going to come from the bottom up when we in the grassroots get mad enough to make it happen.

Get mad. Stay mad. Now, in our anger we do not sin, but anger can be a powerful and virtuous motivator when under control. Like when a mamma grizzly is angry that a predator threatens her babies. Like when a father is angry that perpetrator threatens his family. Like when a loving but holy God is angry at what sin has done to His creation.

The system is counting on our complacency. And if we're being honest we have to admit to ourselves it has every reason to. But we've always been the ones in charge. We've always out-numbered them. We've just been unwilling to act like it.

Now is the time for that action. The clock is ticking on these United States of America. The last, best hope for human freedom this side of Eden is on the brink of becoming a footnote in human history. Do you want to be the generation that has to look our children in the eye and explain why liberty died?

Not on my watch. Who's with me?